CHATGPT SIMPLIFIED

NON-TECH BEGINNERS GUIDE TO UNDERSTANDING AI

LEARN TO CRAFT EFFECTIVE PROMPTS AND CREATE COMPELLING CONTENT

AI EXPLAINED

Copyright © AI Explained 2023

All rights reserved. No part of this book may be reproduced, stored in a retrieval system, or transmitted in any form or by any means—electronic, mechanical, photocopying, recording, or otherwise—without the prior written permission of the publisher, except for brief quotations embodied in critical articles and reviews.

Published by AI Explained

www.aiexplained.ai

For permission requests, contact the publisher

info@aiexplained.ai

Disclaimer: The information contained in this book is for general informational purposes only. The author and publisher make no representation or warranties of any kind, express or implied, about the completeness, accuracy, reliability, suitability, or availability with respect to the book or the information, products, services, or related graphics contained in the book for any purpose. Any reliance you place on such information is therefore strictly at your own risk.

CONTENTS

Introduction — v

1. Board the Rocket — 1
   Getting Started with ChatGPT
2. 5 Easy Steps — 16
   To ChatGPT Mastery
3. The Golden Ticket — 30
   Crafting Effective Prompts
4. Through the Looking Glass — 43
   ChatGPT for Personal and Professional Growth
5. Taming Chaos — 57
   Boost Your Productivity
6. Bag the Bucks — 70
   Earn More with ChatGPT
7. Virtual Theme Park — 82
   Fun with ChatGPT
8. The Moral Maze — 96
   Ethics and A.I.
9. The Future of Possibility — 107
   ChatGPT and Your Future

INTRODUCTION

*AI promises to be the most
transformative technology in history*
– Bill Gates

This from the guy who created Microsoft and revolutionized the world with a desktop computer.

Back in 1975, when Bill Gates and Steve Jobs were just 20 years old, they shared visionary ideas. Gates imagined a future where every household would have a computer. Jobs envisioned a world where computers were small, portable, and accessible to all.

People thought they were nuts!

Today, we can't imagine life without computers, smartphones, the Internet, or Netflix. Technology has truly changed the way we work and live.

Unfortunately, technology hasn't freed us from…

INFORMATION OVERLOAD

Are you swamped with too many projects, an overflowing email inbox, and social media distractions? Are you overwhelmed by a never-ending to-do list, worried about work, and challenged by time management? Do you stress about relationships, finances, and work-life balance?

STOP

Take a deep breath…

And exhale.

Did you know there's a way for you to take control of your life and ease those feelings of anxiety?

I'm not talking about The Force or the Infinity Stones, but something equally as powerful.

CHATGPT

Welcome to ChatGPT, your guide on the path to reclaiming control and finding balance in your life.

Unlocking the power of ChatGPT is like rubbing a magic lamp and unleashing the power of a genie. Just like Aladdin, you've stumbled upon a powerful ally that's ready to help you conquer those projects, organize your email inbox, and overcome distractions from social media.

Here's the best part… ChatGPT isn't limited to granting just three wishes. It's an AI companion that tirelessly works day and night, without ever asking for a vacation in Agrabah.

ChatGPT can help you complete your to-do list, brainstorm work solutions, and prioritize your chaotic daily schedule faster than the Millennium Falcon making the Kessel Run.

Like Obi-Wan Kenobi, ChatGPT empowers you to strengthen your relationships and master your finances. With ChatGPT's guidance, you can achieve harmony between your career and personal life, just as Luke Skywalker found balance between the light and dark sides of The Force.

If you need a boost of creativity, ChatGPT can be your Yoda, guiding you to generate ideas and solutions like a skilled Jedi Master, effortlessly maneuvering through challenges and uncovering the hidden wisdom of The Force.

This book will help you unleash the power of ChatGPT to transform the way you work and live. The possibilities are transformative and we'll explore a myriad of ways to make the most of this fantastic tool.

FROM THE AUTHOR

I'm Richard Rosser, author of *ChatGPT Simplified*, a user-friendly guide that demystifies ChatGPT using everyday language.

Whether you're a non-tech freelancer, aspiring entrepreneur, small business owner, or tech-savvy professional, this book is your companion on an exciting journey to explore ChatGPT. With clear explanations and practical examples, you'll unlock the full potential of this incredible tool and harness its power to revolutionize your life.

BACKGROUND

I'm a filmmaker, author, app developer, and educator. I honed my skills on renowned TV shows, including *Grey's Anatomy*, *Chicago Med*, *This Is Us*, *MacGyver*, and *24*.

I've written award-winning books and taught story workshops to 15,000+ students of all ages. My passion for the creative process led me to develop school curricula that empower students to express themselves through storytelling and conquer their fear of speaking in public.

Beyond my work with students from K-12, I've guest lectured at numerous colleges and universities, including Johns Hopkins, Columbia, and NYU.

DISCOVERING CHATGPT

When ChatGPT was released, it's potential was obvious. I started using the initial version for brainstorming, outlining, research, and content creation.

With subsequent iterations, my fascination grew as I discovered the endless possibilities of this remarkable technology. While I acknowledge ChatGPT's limitations and the risk of misuse, I believe that its positive impact outweighs the negatives.

As an expert in communication, I'm excited to harness the power of ChatGPT. It will revolutionize how we connect and engage with each other. With its ability to create compelling content and craft impactful messages, ChatGPT opens up exciting new options for dynamic communication.

I'm thrilled to help you master ChatGPT to unleash creativity, boost productivity, enhance learning, and transform your interactions. Get ready to explore this revolutionary technology and unlock its extraordinary capabilities!

ONE
BOARD THE ROCKET
GETTING STARTED WITH CHATGPT

Computers are fast, accurate, and stupid
Humans are slow, inaccurate, and brilliant
Together they are powerful beyond imagination
– Albert Einstein

ChatGPT is like the Pete Davidson of the tech world… All over the news, for better or worse.

Elon Musk thinks ChatGPT will destroy humanity. But hold on, don't panic yet. There's a lot of misinformation out there. Some say ChatGPT is Skynet from Terminator. Others liken it to having a personal R2-D2. Which is it? The end of the world or a pocket-sized C3PO?

Consider this… New York City schools banned ChatGPT from all devices and networks on their campuses. Maybe they think ChatGPT is the Voldemort of technology. Apparently, NYC administrators and teachers are worried that students will use ChatGPT to cheat on their homework.

I've got news for them… Students have been cheating since the dawn of time. Whether passing notes or copying off a classmate's paper, cheating isn't a new phenomenon. A cheater's gonna cheat.

Instead of banning ChatGPT, we need to embrace it, teach it, use it. With ChatGPT, students can explore original ideas and unique perspectives. They can use it to amplify their creativity and originality. Instead of fearing ChatGPT, let's use it as a tool for growth, development, and expression.

As Master Yoda once said, "Fear is the path to the dark side. Fear leads to anger, anger leads to hate, hate leads to suffering." Don't let fear hold you back from unlocking the full potential of ChatGPT.

HISTORY AND TECHNOLOGY

Throughout history, technological advancements have had the potential for good and evil. From the printing press to the Internet, there have always been those who use new inventions for nefarious purposes. Take books for example. From the first printing of *The Gutenberg Bible* to the latest issue of the *National Enquirer*, the technology of the printed word shows us the very best and worst of humanity.

ChatGPT is no different. It's a powerful tool that can be used for good or evil, just like any other technology. So, let's use it responsibly, like Tony Stark with his Iron Man suit, and we'll all be okay. For the vast majority of people, ChatGPT is a tool for good. It can create amazing content, boost productivity, and help tackle global issues like hunger, homelessness, and climate change. Like The Force - there's a light side and a dark side.

MAGICAL POSSIBILITIES

In this book, we'll embark on an epic adventure to unlock the magical possibilities when you harness the power of ChatGPT. Imagine finding a secret map to a treasure trove of knowledge and potential.

Get ready to dive deep into the rabbit hole of self-discovery, because ChatGPT is here to guide you on an exhilarating journey of personal and professional transformation. It's like the Ben Kenobi of technology, wise and full of insights. You'll uncover hidden truths about yourself and tap into your inner abilities.

So, fasten your seatbelt and prepare for a wild ride. Say goodbye to the mundane and hello to the extraordinary! Get ready to unleash your creativity and conquer the challenges that stand in your way. Together, we'll make the impossible possible and create a future that's straight out of our wildest dreams.

ABOUT CHATGPT

Let me tell you about ChatGPT - the new Artificial Intelligence program that's like the lovechild of Siri and the Oracle of Delphi. ChatGPT is an AI-powered text generator that can understand human language and respond to your questions in a way that makes you feel like you're talking to an actual person.

And boy, does it have personality! ChatGPT can be sassy, witty, or empathetic, depending on your mood. It's like having a BFF who's always there to cheer you up, give you advice, or just shoot the breeze. Plus, ChatGPT is always up for a funny joke, so you know it's got a great sense of humor.

SIMPLICITY

Here's the best part… You don't need to be a tech wizard to use ChatGPT. Just type a question and ChatGPT responds with an answer that's smart, informative, and maybe even a little bit cheeky.

So whether you need help with a presentation, want to vent about your boss, or just feel like chatting about the latest TikTok trend, ChatGPT has your back. It's like having an assistant, therapist, and comedian all rolled into one. And it's available 24/7, so you can chat whenever and wherever you want. Join the ChatGPT revolution and experience the magic of Artificial Intelligence for yourself!

HOW CHATGPT WORKS

ChatGPT is an advanced AI communication program (also known as a model) that has the remarkable ability to generate text that closely resembles human writing. Let's analyze the moniker ChatGPT…

The word *Chat* refers to how ChatGPT works as a conversational model. It's designed to *chat* with users, just like you would with another person. It responds to questions in a natural, conversational way. The goal is to make it feel like you're having a real conversation.

GPT is short for *Generative Pre-trained Transformer*.

GENERATIVE

The term *generative* means the model can create, or generate, new content. ChatGPT is text-based so it generates text responses to your questions. Other types of generative AI models generate images, music, videos, and even entire virtual worlds.

PRE-TRAINED

Pre-trained means the model has gone through a training process before it's ready to use. By the time you interact with the model, it's been trained on a massive amount of text called the *Common Crawl*, which is made up of billions of web pages including blog posts, *Wikipedia* entries, discussion forums, and social media posts. This pre-training gives ChatGPT the ability to understand patterns, relationships, and how language works.

TRANSFORMER

Transformer is a type of software architecture the model is built on. It's a type of deep learning technology that's really good at understanding language and making connections between words and sentences. Transformers have made a big impact on tasks like understanding and generating text.

SUMMARY

To sum it up, a *Generative Pre-trained Transformer* (GPT) is a language model that has been trained on lots of text data using a transformer architecture. It can generate text that sounds natural and makes sense based on the instructions you've given. This makes it a powerful tool for tasks like writing, completing text, and understanding language.

TEXT GENERATION

Think of pre-training as a language school for robots. During pre-training, ChatGPT learns to predict the sequence of words in a sentence. It's like playing a never-ending game of *Mad Libs*, except instead of filling in the blanks with silly words, you're teaching a robot how to talk.

ChatGPT utilizes a technique called unsupervised learning, which means that the model is fine-tuned for specific tasks, like language translation or question answering. Imagine your robot getting a Ph.D. in a particular subject - suddenly, it's an expert in everything from French to physics.

This unsupervised learning technique allows ChatGPT to generate text as though it was written by a human. Similar to robot voice assistants, but way smarter and less annoying. The model is so good that it can even understand context, something that many humans struggle with.

UNDERSTANDING LANGUAGE

Because ChatGPT is trained on massive amounts of text, it has a deep understanding of the structure and syntax of language. Imagine a robot who's fluent in every language on Earth - except instead of learning from books or classes, it learned from a massive collection of text. This understanding allows it to generate content that is grammatically correct and contextually appropriate.

But, that's just the beginning. ChatGPT also uses a software device called attention mechanisms to focus on the most relevant parts of your question. Like a psychic who knows exactly what you're going to say, even before you say it... This allows ChatGPT to generate accurate responses and match the tone of your questions and conversations.

Here's where things get really cool. ChatGPT translates text with a high level of accuracy. Gone are the days when you'd end up saying something inappropriate when using a language translator. ChatGPT is ready and able to help you communicate with people across the globe.

CONTENT CREATION

If you're feeling creative, ChatGPT generates text that is stylistically and thematically consistent with a given question. Consider having a robot ghostwriter who can write a poem or news article at the drop of a hat. ChatGPT is your very own muse - like having a co-author who knows exactly what you're trying to say.

Perhaps the most magical thing about ChatGPT is its ability to personalize responses based on your previous interactions. Consider it a robot friend who listens to what you say and remembers everything you've said before. This makes ChatGPT more than just a language model - it's essentially a friend who's always there to chat - whether you're looking for advice, information, or just some good old-fashioned small talk.

Overall, the magic of ChatGPT lies in its ability to understand and generate human-like language. As AI technology evolves, you can expect to see even more magic from ChatGPT and other advanced language models. Maybe one day you'll even teach ChatGPT how to perform magic tricks.

CREATIVITY

ChatGPT is like the James Bond of AI - sleek and sophisticated with a range of gadgets and tricks up its sleeve to engage in creative conversations. Decoding the secrets of ChatGPT gives you a glimpse into its inner workings and reveals the magic that makes it such a powerful tool for human-machine interaction.

I have to admit, ChatGPT is a bit of a genius. By analyzing previous conversations and interactions, it builds a personalized profile based on the way you communicate. ChatGPT uses the profile to generate responses that are ever more accurate and relevant. Imagine having a personal assistant that gets to know you better and better over time, except this one doesn't complain about making copies.

And let's not forget the pièce de résistance - ChatGPT's potential for creativity and innovation. It's essentially a modern-day Shakespeare, capable of generating language in a wide range of styles and genres. Whether you're looking to write a blog post or craft the perfect tweet, ChatGPT provides inspiration and ideas that are tailor-made for your needs.

To decode the secrets of ChatGPT, approach it with a sense of discovery and a willingness to experiment. Try engaging in conversations and see where it takes you. Who knows, you might just uncover a few more of its secrets along the way.

CHATGPT IS GOOD AT...

Are you ready for a whimsical exploration of ChatGPT's talents? You'll laugh, you'll cry, you'll wonder why you didn't use ChatGPT sooner.

- **The Know-It-All** - ChatGPT is a digital smarty-pants that dishes out answers on everything from ancient history to rocket science.

- **Text Generator Extraordinaire** - As a language model, ChatGPT churns out coherent, contextually spot-on, and grammatically impeccable text, putting your high school English teacher to shame.
- **Chatty Cathy** - ChatGPT, the life of the virtual party, engages in natural-sounding conversations that make it perfect for chatbot applications or virtual assistants.
- **Creative Genius** - The Shakespeare of Silicon Valley, ChatGPT spins tales, pens poetry, and crafts creative writing that would make Mark Twain jealous.
- **Master Condenser** - ChatGPT condenses lengthy text, articles, or documents into bite-sized nuggets of wisdom, preserving the juicy bits and all-important context.
- **Language Chameleon** - ChatGPT leaps between languages, translating text with the ease of a babbling polyglot.
- **The Mood Detector** - ChatGPT peers into the emotional depths of text, determining if it's brimming with sunshine, drowning in sorrow, or lounging in stoicism.
- **Problem-Solving Guru** - ChatGPT tosses out potential solutions and strategies for life's many challenges, like a digital fortune cookie full of helpful advice.
- **Idea Factory** - ChatGPT generates new ideas and concepts on-demand, making it the ultimate partner in your next brainstorming session.
- **Coding Sidekick** - ChatGPT swoops in to save the day, tackling coding questions, debugging pesky issues, and serving up sample code in a variety of programming languages.

As AI technology evolves, you can expect to see even more mind-blowing capabilities from ChatGPT. It's like watching a science fiction movie come to life before your very eyes. The possibilities for communication, knowledge retrieval, and creativity are staggering.

INFINITE IMAGINATION

One of the most impressive aspects of ChatGPT's infinite imagination is its ability to generate highly specific language based on context. Imagine a superpower that allows you to explore complex subjects and generate highly personalized responses. No topic is too obscure or too complex for ChatGPT's infinite imagination to handle.

- **Mythical Creatures** - Ask ChatGPT about mythical creatures, including Sasquatch, the Loch Ness Monster, and the Chupacabra, as well as the legends and folklore surrounding them.
- **Time Travel** - Users have inquired about the feasibility of time travel, multiple dimensions, and the many-worlds interpretation of quantum mechanics.
- **Extraterrestrial Life** - ChatGPT has fielded numerous questions about the existence of extraterrestrial life, UFO sightings, and the potential for contact with alien civilizations.
- **Creative Culinary Creations** - Ask ChatGPT about strange food combinations like insect-based cuisine, durian fruit, or unconventional pizza toppings.
- **Obscure Historical Events** - Many users have asked ChatGPT to research lesser-known events or individuals from history, such as bizarre inventions, strange wars, or eccentric personalities.

If you're a writer, artist, or someone who loves exploring new ideas and concepts, ChatGPT's infinite imagination is like a dream come true. As you feed it questions and topics, you'll unlock a limitless array of creative possibilities, allowing you to explore new ideas and concepts in ways that would be impossible otherwise.

TOP SECRET INSIGHTS

ChatGPT uses all kinds of fancy techniques including attention mechanisms and language models to understand your questions and generate responses that are relevant and tailored to your needs.

It's also a master of feedback. As ChatGPT engages in conversations with you, it's constantly learning and improving its language model, using your feedback to become even more accurate and relevant. It's like a linguistic chameleon, adapting to your every whim and desire.

However, as powerful as ChatGPT may be, it's still just a machine and it may not always understand the nuances of human communication, so you need to approach conversations with a healthy dose of caution. After all, you don't want to end up in a linguistic labyrinth with no way out!

Overall, the world of ChatGPT conversations is fascinating and ever-evolving. In the future, you should expect to see more sophisticated capabilities and a deeper understanding of how humans and machines communicate with each other. So raise a glass to ChatGPT, the magical machine that's changing the way you work. Cheers!

COMBINING GENRES

Want to know the scoop on ChatGPT's hidden gems? This natural language processing tool is essentially a treasure chest just waiting to be opened, full of linguistic riches beyond your wildest dreams.

First up, there's ChatGPT's ability to generate language in any style or genre you can think of. Want a sonnet about avocado toast? ChatGPT's got you covered. Need a scientific paper on the mating habits of unicorns? No problem. But that's not all! ChatGPT can also learn and adapt to your personal preferences over time. Just like your favorite coffee shop barista who knows your order before you even say it. Except, without the latte art (that's MidJourney's job!).

And here's the kicker… ChatGPT is paving the way for a whole new level of human-machine interaction, like a new friend who talks to you about anything and everything under the sun. It won't even get mad when you start rambling about your ex.

CHATGPT IS BAD AT...

Step right up! I now present the amusing underbelly of ChatGPT. A delightful look at its quirks and foibles:

- **Vague Dilemmas** - When faced with ambiguous or murky questions, ChatGPT scratches its virtual head, struggling to serve up a satisfactory answer.
- **The Time Warp** - ChatGPT was trained on the *Common Crawl* through September 2021, so its knowledge is sketchy after that date. Because of this, ChatGPT might be a bit behind the times, missing the latest gossip, breakthroughs, and news worldwide.
- **Bias Blunder** - Despite best intentions, ChatGPT may still churn out biased outputs, accidentally perpetuating stereotypes or spreading misinformation.
- **Hallucinations** - ChatGPT occasionally slips up, dishing out inaccurate or misleading tidbits, especially if its training data was a bit off. AI experts call this *hallucinating*.
- **Context Conundrum** - Complex context and intricate topic relationships may trip up ChatGPT.
- **Long-Winded Inconsistency** - As a conversation drones on, ChatGPT might lose its bearings, providing inconsistent responses like a forgetful grandparent.
- **Sarcasm Struggle** - Detecting and responding to sarcasm, irony, or humor can baffle ChatGPT, leaving it scrambling to find an appropriate reaction.

- **Privacy Problems** - ChatGPT, like an overly curious neighbor, may unintentionally coax users to spill sensitive or personal details.

Despite these limitations, ChatGPT is ever-evolving and improving. Researchers continue to tackle these challenges with gusto, striving to perfect this digital marvel.

Before we go any further, let's get you signed up and logged on to ChatGPT.

CREATE A CHATGPT ACCOUNT

Step 1 - Got to https://chat.openai.com/auth/login

Step 2 - Click Sign Up

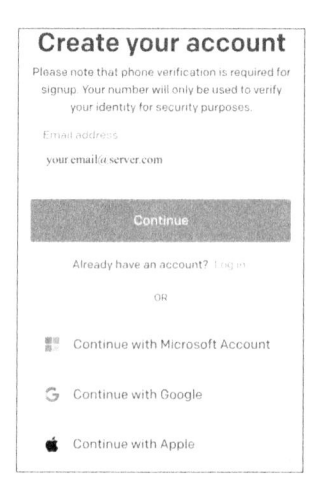

Step 3 - Sign up using your email address or continue with your Microsoft, Google, or Apple account.

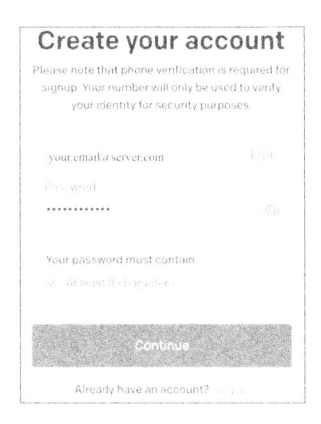

Step 4 - If you choose to sign up with your email, enter a password. You'll receive a verification email.

Step 5 - Check your email inbox for the OpenAI verification email. Click on *Verify Email Address*. Return to the Log in page and log in using your email and password.

Step 6 - Enter your first name, last name, and birthday. Click *Continue*.

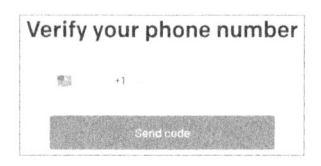

Step 7 - Whichever sign up method you choose, phone verification is required. Enter your number and click *Send code*.

Step 8 - Enter the 6-digit code you receive on your phone. You should be returned to the home page where you can log in with your email and password (or Microsoft/Google/Apple info).

LOG IN TO CHATGPT

Once you've created an account, here's how you log in.

Step 1 - Go to the ChatGPT log in page.

https://chat.openai.com/auth/login

Step 2 - Click *Log in*.

Step 3 - Choose your login method.

Email Address - Enter your email and password. Click *Continue*.

Microsoft - Follow the instructions to log in with your Microsoft account.

Google - Follow the instructions to log in with your Google account.

Apple - Follow the instructions to log in with your Apple account.

UPGRADE TO CHATGPT PLUS

As of publication, you can use ChatGPT for free. You can upgrade to ChatGPT Plus for $20 per month which includes the following:

- Access to ChatGPT 4.0
- Available even when demand is high
- Faster response speed
- Priority access to new features

CONCLUSION

ChatGPT is the gateway to AI just like web browsers are the portal to the internet. Think of ChatGPT as the bouncer at the door to the club of the future, making sure you're cool enough to come in and party with the adults. And just like web browsers, ChatGPT has come a long way since its early days.

In fact, ChatGPT's history is a wild ride, full of twists, turns, and more than a few "wait, what?" moments. From its humble beginnings as a basic language model, ChatGPT has evolved into a sophisticated AI tool. It's like the little language model that could, but then got an upgrade and became the language model that definitely can!

KEY TAKEAWAYS FROM CHAPTER 1

- ChatGPT is an AI-powered text generator
- ChatGPT translates text into numerous languages
- ChatGPT can engage in virtual conversations
- ChatGPT has the ability to understand context
- ChatGPT generates language in any style or genre
- ChatGPT has limitations including bias, inaccurate output, and limited knowledge after September 2021

Let's explore the 5 Easy Steps to ChatGPT mastery…

TWO
5 EASY STEPS
TO CHATGPT MASTERY

Learn about ChatGPT
Otherwise, you're going to be a dinosaur in three years
– Mark Cuban

Are you ready to harness the power of ChatGPT and join the ranks of those who have mastered the art of AI-Assisted Conversation? Well, step right up, and let me tell you about the 5 Easy Steps that will have you chatting like a pro in no time!

First, you gotta **learn**. This step is all about getting to know your new chat buddy. Like anything, learning ChatGPT takes enthusiasm, dedication, and patience. You wouldn't head down a black diamond slope on your first run down a new mountain, would you? Well, maybe you would, but chances are good you'd end up in traction. Same with ChatGPT. You're learning a new skill so it'll take some time, but believe me, it's gonna be worth it!

Once you've learned the basics, it's time to **apply** your newfound knowledge. This is where things get fun! You'll use ChatGPT to have all sorts of interesting and entertaining conversations. And don't worry, I'll give you plenty of tips and tricks for how to keep the chat flowing smoothly.

But you can't just chat blindly. You need to **assess** the situation, understand the context, and make sure you're not confusing your chat partner. That's where the real mastery comes in.

Once you've assessed the situation, it's time to **refine** your technique. Take a critical look at your conversations and figure out what works and what doesn't. It's like going back through your browser history and deleting all those embarrassing Google searches from five years ago.

The last step… **repeat**. Let's be honest, you're never going to finish learning about ChatGPT. Sure, you'll get better and better, but ChatGPT is constantly evolving so there will always be new ways to use it. Keep chatting, keep refining, and keep learning!

BENEFITS

With ChatGPT at your fingertips, you can do all sorts of amazing things. You can have conversations in multiple languages, get help with social media posts, and even use ChatGPT to update your to-do list! Plus, with the impending zombie apocalypse, ChatGPT might soon be the only friend you've got left in this crazy world. Yikes!

Here's the thing that blows my mind - ChatGPT sounds human. Have you heard some of the conversations that people have had? It's wild! And that's because of the incredible way ChatGPT processes information and generates responses. It's a robot brain that's constantly working to make your life easier and more entertaining.

As I mentioned, it's going to take some effort to learn to use this new technology. But my 5 Easy Steps will help you master ChatGPT in no time!

Before diving in to learn about ChatGPT, let's take a brief tour of the ChatGPT screen.

18   CHATGPT SIMPLIFIED

SCREEN TOUR

When you log on to ChatGPT, at the bottom of the screen is a dialogue box. To start a conversation, type a question where it says *Send a message* and hit enter. ChatGPT will generate a response. Continue the conversation by entering another question.

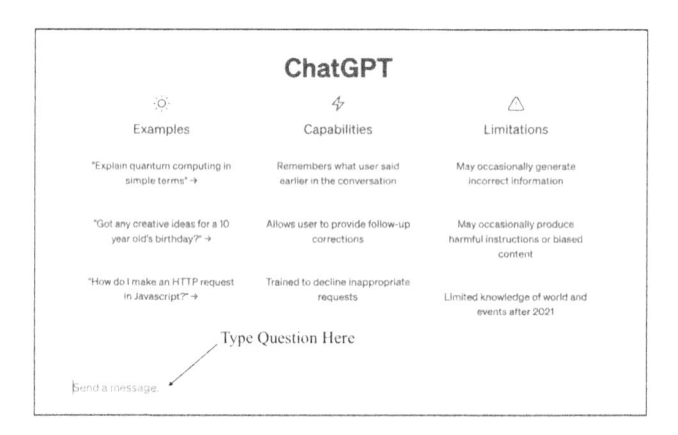

After ChatGPT generates a response, give feedback or generate a 2nd response by pressing *Regenerate response*. .

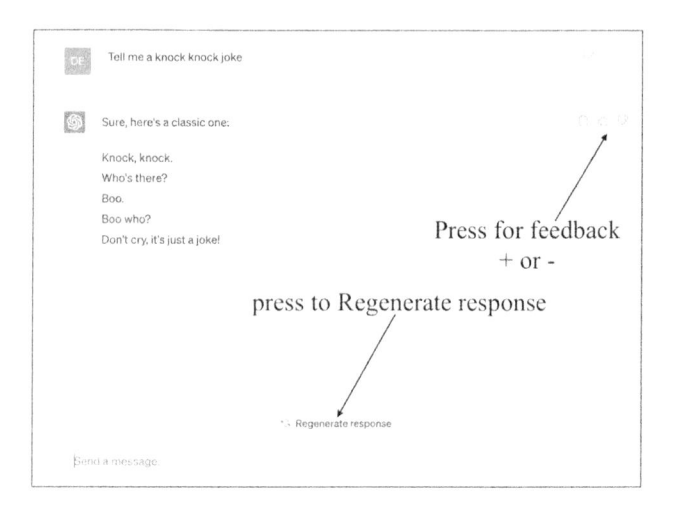

After ChatGPT generates a 2nd response, choose between output versions, give feedback, or generate another response.

5 EASY STEPS   19

[Screenshot showing a ChatGPT knock-knock joke exchange with annotations: "Choose between output versions", "Press for feedback", and "Generate another response"]

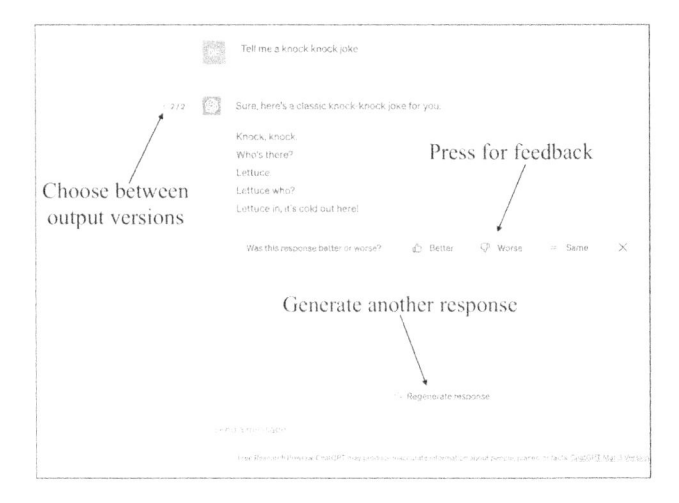

To rename or delete the current chat, press the pen or trashcan in the upper left corner. To create a new chat, press *New chat* in the upper left corner.

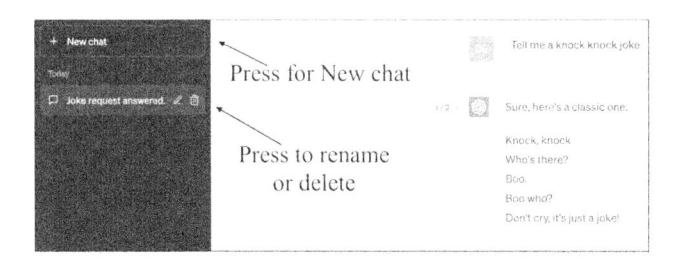

[Screenshot showing the ChatGPT sidebar with annotations: "Press for New chat" and "Press to rename or delete"]

When in doubt, experiment. Don't know what a button does? Click it to find out. If you get stuck, ask ChatGPT for help.

STEP 1 - LEARN

Are you ready for a rollercoaster ride of cutting-edge technology? Well, hold on tight, because ChatGPT is new and changing every day, hour, minute - it's like trying to keep up with the Kardashians, only less exhausting (and hopefully with fewer scandals). And because ChatGPT is still evolving, there's a bit of a learning curve. But it's like learning how to surf - you're gonna fall off a few times before you ride the wave.

While you're learning, keep in mind… Everyone else is learning right along with you. Sure, some folks started experimenting with ChatGPT last year so they're a bit ahead, but everyone is struggling to keep up with the evolving technology and new developments.

It's easy to get overwhelmed. But, like the fable of the tortoise and the hare. Slow and steady wins the race. Also, remember that ChatGPT is actually its own best learning resource. Lost in the AI maze? No worries, you can always ask ChatGPT for directions. It's like having an instruction manual with its own instruction manual.

Wanna know the cool part? ChatGPT is constantly learning from its interactions with users, so it gets better and better every day. Sort of like how you're learning about it. And if you want to master ChatGPT, you've got to experiment and try new things. You got this! Take a deep breath and enjoy the ride.

LEARNING STYLES

Let's talk about different styles of learning. Some people love to read, others prefer videos, and some thrive in group discussions. Different learning modes help reinforce your understanding and keep things interesting. It's like a buffet for your brain! And don't forget to set goals. Having measurable goals will motivate you to keep learning and improve your skills. It's like having a personal brain trainer.

First up, webinars. These are like those Zoom meetings you're always late to but with way more exciting content. You can attend online sessions hosted by experts where they discuss ChatGPT and all its cool capabilities. Imagine belonging to a secret club of ChatGPT insiders! Most webinars are hosted by companies, but there are many free webinars available for ChatGPT newbies.

Next, lectures. These are like college classes but without overpriced textbooks and questionable dining hall food. You can attend talks on ChatGPT at universities and educational institutions, where professors discuss ChatGPT and its impact. It's like getting a front-row seat at the *Consumer Electronics Show*.

VISUAL LEARNERS

If you're a visual learner, YouTube tutorials might be your jam. You'll find videos of experts demonstrating how ChatGPT works and sharing their experiences working with the technology. It's like having your own personal ChatGPT coach.

Online courses are another great option. You can enroll in courses specifically focused on ChatGPT and other related technologies. Imagine taking a class without the fear of getting called on by the teacher. Online courses are great options if you love learning at your own pace at home, on a lunch break, or during your daily commute.

Research papers might not sound like the most exciting way to learn, but trust me, they're worth checking out. You can read about how it works, its capabilities, and potential applications. While the language is difficult in these papers, you can always use ChatGPT to summarize the writing! Just plug the paper into ChatGPT and let it do the reading for you.

ONLINE COMMUNITIES

Don't forget about online communities and forums! You can join groups where experts discuss ChatGPT, share their experiences, and answer questions from the community. Imagine joining a secret club of ChatGPT enthusiasts who all speak the same language.

Finally, there are conferences focused on ChatGPT. Similar to ComicCon, but for techies. You can attend workshops and meet other ChatGPT enthusiasts. It's like being at the coolest tech party ever, with free swag!

Optimally, you'll combine a mixture of different learning resources. And given that ChatGPT is constantly evolving, there's always something new to discover. The more you learn about ChatGPT, the more you'll learn about yourself.

STEP 2 - APPLY

Now that you've learned something about ChatGPT, it's time to apply your newfound knowledge to gain some experience. There are a number of ways for you to apply what you've learned. The best approach is to dive right in and start experimenting.

The simplest thing you can do to get started is to ask ChatGPT some questions. Start with basic questions about history, science, or pop culture and get instant answers. It's like having your own personal Google search engine but with more personality. Give these questions a shot…

Did George Washington really have wooden teeth?
How do animals use camouflage to outsmart predators?
Darth Vader opens a restaurant. What's his signature dish?

Next, is text completion. Use ChatGPT to complete sentences or paragraphs. Try these questions on for size…

After a long day at work, I decided to relax by ___
When I woke up this morning, my pet goldfish tried to ___
I accidentally walked into a room full of ___. Boy, was that a sight!

Now let's talk content creation. Here are some questions I created for one of my first experiments. Enter each line as a separate question and see how ChatGPT responds differently to each variation…

Write a paragraph about finding a lost dog
In the style of Shakespeare
In the style of Toni Morrison
In the style of Virginia Woolf
In the style of Edgar Allen Poe
In the style of Hunter S. Thompson

In each case, ChatGPT will respond with a simple paragraph about a dog, written in the style, cadence, and emotion of each author.

EXPERIMENT

You might also ask ChatGPT to describe your favorite book, song, or movie. See what happens when you ask it to create a Twitter post. Pretty cool having a digital writing coach to help spark your creativity, right? Use ChatGPT to generate questions for creative writing exercises and get those creative juices flowing with your own personal AI muse. Give these questions a try…

Generate questions for creative writing exercises
Describe the song Watermelon Sugar by Harry Styles
Create a Twitter post about Avengers Endgame with hashtags

Try engaging in a conversation with ChatGPT to improve your communication skills and enhance your ability to engage in meaningful discussions. These questions are perfect…

Start a conversation about talking animals
Start a conversation about personal theme songs
Start a conversation about swapping lives with a TV character

ChatGPT is an excellent resource for content creators. Use it to help you brainstorm ideas, generate story plots, or develop characters. It can serve as a writing companion and offer suggestions during the writing process. Feeling uninspired, try these questions…

List some character traits of a villain
Outline a plot for an action movie about trees
What are some ideas for a romantic comedy set in Bali?

What about text summarization and content recommendation? Text summarization is like having your own personal SparkNotes. Use ChatGPT to summarize a short article or condense a report into a few key bullet points.

Content recommendation is like having your own Netflix algorithm. Use ChatGPT to recommend articles or videos based on your interests. You'll love having your own private ChatGPT concierge.

Summarize the following: [cut and paste text]
Recommend movies that my dog and I can watch together
Summarize and format the results as bullet points: [cut and paste text]

These examples just scratch the surface of applying your newfound knowledge about ChatGPT. Whether you're researching George Washington's dentures or generating character traits of a villain, there are numerous ways to apply your knowledge. So, go forth and explore this wild and wonderful technology!

STEP 3 - ASSESS

Now that you've spent some time test-driving ChatGPT, it's time to take a look in the digital mirror and assess your skills. It may not be pretty, but that's okay because you can always take another lap around the test track.

How are you feeling? Satisfied, frustrated, overwhelmed? Probably a bit of each, right? Reflect on what you've learned during your first dive into ChatGPT.

Try some self-reflection. Did you crush it or did it crush you? Think about what went well and what didn't. It's like a therapy session but for robots.

I recommend keeping a journal handy - hardcopy or online - where you can list what worked, what failed, and what you're confused by. Consider having ChatGPT track your progress in a saved conversation thread!

PEER FEEDBACK

Now, onto peer feedback. Share your work with a friend or colleague who knows their way around ChatGPT and ask for their opinion. Do they find your output charming or cringey? It's like submitting your stand-up comedy routine, but instead of laughs, you get feedback on your chat banter.

Take some time to assess your experience with ChatGPT. Embrace the awkwardness and learn from your mistakes. Who knows, you might just become the ChatGPT MVP of your office!

One fun way to assess your learning journey is to turn the tables and give ChatGPT a taste of its own medicine. That's right, I'm talking about the ChatGPT feedback loop…

THE CHATGPT FEEDBACK LOOP

Here's how it works: Start by engaging ChatGPT in a conversation and then ask it to assess its own accuracy or responsiveness. Then, sit back and watch as ChatGPT tries to evaluate its own performance without breaking down into a pile of circuits and wires. Here are some questions you can use…

How well did you respond to the above input?
How accurate was the information you generated?
Create a rubric for evaluating your responses and grade yourself

Take the self-evaluations with a grain of salt. ChatGPT has been known to exhibit an inflated ego when assessing its own work.

Remember, you can also provide suggestions to improve ChatGPT's output. Maybe ChatGPT could use a little more pizzazz in its responses or perhaps you want it to generate output with more slang or pop culture references. Try these questions…

Rewrite with sarcasm and irony
Infuse the passage with New York City street slang
Rework and include pop culture references from the 1990s

The ChatGPT feedback loop is a fun and interactive way to assess your learning journey.

STEP 4 - REFINE

After you've taken your first steps into the wild world of ChatGPT, you'll be itching to refine your skills and become a true master. Have no fear, here are some simple ways to refine your knowledge and experience.

First, practice, practice, practice! Anytime you learn something new, practice is key. So, get typing and start using ChatGPT for various tasks like answering questions, text completion, or content creation.

MORE FEEDBACK

Next, seek more feedback from others who have experience using ChatGPT. Expand your feedback group to include members of online communities like Reddit or Discord.

Acquire additional information and stay up-to-date with new research and developments. This might involve reading research papers or following experts on social media where they're sharing the latest ChatGPT developments. Twitter is especially useful for this. Research papers can be difficult to read, so consider truncated versions of research like *Two Minute Papers* on Youtube.

Identify specific areas for improvement by reflecting on your experience using ChatGPT. Maybe you struggle with generating high-quality output or understanding the model. Maybe you just can't get it to stop calling you "Dave". Whatever the issue, identify the problem and tackle it head-on. If you get stuck, remember to ask ChatGPT for help!

STEP 5 - REPEAT

Becoming a ChatGPT Sensei requires practice, persistence, and repetition! Just like a martial arts master perfects their moves through countless repetitions, you can hone your ChatGPT skills by using the program on a daily basis.

Repeat conversations with variations on a theme, explore different topics, and experiment with unique questions. Each interaction is an opportunity to learn and grow. Embrace the process, even if you hit a few speed bumps along the way.

As you regenerate responses, you'll gain insights into ChatGPT's capabilities and limitations. You'll uncover its strengths and discover clever workarounds for its quirks. With each repetition, you'll become more attuned to the nuances of the model, guiding it with finesse and creativity.

So, my aspiring ChatGPT Sensei, remember the 5 easy steps to ChatGPT mastery... **Learn**, **apply**, **assess**, **refine**, and **repeat**.

Embrace the journey, celebrate your progress, and you'll evolve into a true master of ChatGPT.

TIPS AND TRICKS

Make the most of your learning experience with ChatGPT.

- **Reflect -** After each session, take a moment to reflect on what you've learned. Work to cement it in your brain. Think of this as flexing your brain muscles - the more you do it, the stronger they'll get.
- **Practice -** Given that ChatGPT is ever-evolving, you may never reach perfection. That doesn't mean you shouldn't practice. The more you practice the skills you've acquired, the more they'll seamlessly integrate into your workflow.
- **Teach -** There's an adage that goes… *The best way to learn something is to teach it.* Teaching someone else is a fantastic way to reinforce your understanding of the material and you'll have a chance to show off your newfound knowledge and impress your friends (or at least your mom).
- **Spaced Repetition -** This is where you review material at increasing intervals. Think of it like interval training for your brain - you're gradually building up your endurance for remembering all that ChatGPT goodness.

- **Take Breaks -** You don't want to burn out by going too hard too fast. Take some time to relax and recharge. You'll return to the material refreshed and ready to repeat.
- **Your Brain -** Here's a cool fact about your brain... It doesn't stop working, even when you want it to. Go for a run, a walk, or a bike ride. Your brain will continue processing what you've learned.
- **Fresh Perspective -** When you return to your computer, you may find that new insights and fresh perspectives have emerged, fueling your creative potential and enhancing your problem-solving abilities.

With these tips and tricks, you'll be reinforcing your ChatGPT skills like nobody's business. Get out there and show ChatGPT who's boss!

RECAP

You're absolutely crushing it, like a Jedi Padawan learning to harness the power of the Force. And just like Master Yoda, ChatGPT is here to help you hone your skills so you can become a true Jedi Master of text generation.

But let's be real, this whole process might be a bit overwhelming. Don't worry. Slow and steady wins the race. Remember, everyone else is still learning about ChatGPT too. It's like a big party where everyone's trying to learn the electric slide and nobody knows what they're doing.

Be patient with yourself and commit to understanding the technology's capabilities and limitations. Webinars, online courses, and YouTube videos will help you grasp the basics. Experimenting with different uses of ChatGPT, such as text completion and content creation, will help you apply your understanding and build proficiency.

Assessing your progress is crucial to refining skills and improving performance. Seeking feedback from peers, friends, and online communities can offer a valuable perspective on your work with

ChatGPT. Additionally, engaging in self-reflection will help identify areas for improvement and further development.

Refining your ChatGPT skills involves a commitment to practice, seeking feedback, and staying current with the latest developments. By utilizing resources such as research papers and social media, you can stay up-to-date and deepen your understanding of ChatGPT.

Repeating what you've learned, applied, assessed, and refined will help reinforce your understanding and deepen your knowledge. Repetition solidifies new information in your memory, making it more readily accessible when you need it. Just like practicing a musical instrument or sport, repeating what you've learned helps to reinforce neural connections, improving retention and recall.

CONCLUSION

Remember, learning with ChatGPT is an ongoing process because the program is continuously evolving. So don't be afraid to experiment, try new things, and refine your skills. Who knows? Maybe you'll become a ChatGPT wizard, able to conjure up perfect questions. In the meantime, keep practicing, keep learning, and keep having fun.

KEY TAKEAWAYS FROM CHAPTER 2

- There are 5 Easy Steps to Mastering ChatGPT
- Step 1 - **Learn** about ChatGPT
- Step 2 - **Apply** your knowledge
- Step 3 - **Assess** your experience
- Step 4 - **Refine** your skills
- Step 5 - **Repeat** steps 1-4
- Honing your experience is a journey, not a destination

Up next, crafting effective prompts…

THREE
THE GOLDEN TICKET
CRAFTING EFFECTIVE PROMPTS

ChatGPT is going to make us even more human
– Ginni Rometty

There's a popular belief that ChatGPT will be the death of individuality. Critics argue that widespread adoption of ChatGPT for content creation, emails, and blog posts, will result in a society where all forms of communication blend into monotonous mush. They fear that reliance on ChatGPT will eliminate originality, reducing humanity to a hoard of zombie-like communicators.

I have a contrary opinion... I believe that creative individuals who learn to use ChatGPT will amplify their originality and stand out from the crowd. Instead of blindly relying on ChatGPT to churn out generic content, savvy users will use the technology to enhance their unique style and flair. While it's true that ChatGPT has the potential to make us all sound like robots, it can also be used to bring out the best in our creative selves.

Consider *The Hunger Games*. All of the tributes have access to the same arsenal of weapons, yet it's the ones with skill and creativity who emerge victorious. Think of ChatGPT as your personal array of content creation tools. Similar to how Katniss Everdeen honed her abilities to become the ultimate survivor, you too can cultivate and refine your skills with ChatGPT to evolve into a master content creator.

But let's be real, we're not all Katniss-level badasses. Some of us need a little more guidance and support, which is why we **learn** and **apply**. After practicing with ChatGPT, you'll have the skill to unleash the magic of AI to create content that sets you apart. Don't worry, ChatGPT won't turn you into a robotic copycat. It's not like *The Stepford Wives* where everyone looks and acts the same. With the right approach, ChatGPT will amplify your uniqueness and originality. Think of it as adding some spice to your already awesome recipe.

EXPLORE

Approach ChatGPT with an open mind and a hunger for knowledge. Explore its features, play around with it, and don't be afraid to get creative. ChatGPT is your playground and it's okay to stumble and make mistakes. Learning takes time. So, if you don't see immediate progress, don't bum out. Take a break and remember that everyone learns at their own pace.

Embrace the power of ChatGPT, and remember to use it wisely. It's just like Uncle Ben said in *Spider-Man*, "With great power comes great responsibility." But instead of slinging webs and fighting crime, you'll be slinging words and creating content that sets you apart!

PROMPTS

To use ChatGPT effectively, you need to ask it questions, which are commonly referred to as "prompts" in the tech world. A ChatGPT prompt is like a magic incantation that summons the AI creative muses. At its most basic level, a prompt is a question or statement that's designed to inspire or provoke a response. Visualize throwing a pebble into a pond and watching the ripples spread outwards. That's the essence of a prompt.

But prompts aren't just limited to writing or creative endeavors. They can be used for anything, from brainstorming and problem-solving to generating Excel formulas and computer code.

A good prompt should be clear, concise, and specific. It should provide enough direction to get ChatGPT's creative juices flowing, but not so much that it stifles originality. It's like preparing for a session of *Dungeons and Dragons* - you want to provide your players with sufficient background and context to engage in the adventure while leaving ample space for improvisation and unexpected twists.

Prompts can take many forms, from simple words or phrases to complex scenarios. And let's not forget about the power of a good prompt to unlock hidden talents and ideas. Sometimes, all it takes is a little nudge to get your brain working in new and exciting ways.

HOW PROMPTS WORK

ChatGPT prompts are like Sherlock Holmes using AI powers to analyze your words and figure out what you're asking. Imagine a game of 20 questions, except instead of guessing what person, place, or thing you're thinking of, ChatGPT is trying to figure out what information you need.

Here's the kicker - these prompts are based on something called *deep learning*, which means that ChatGPT is constantly evolving like a Pokémon leveling up. The more prompts it receives, the better it gets at understanding human language and providing accurate answers. It's like *The NeverEnding Story* but without the creepy flying dog-dragon thing or the weird horse-sinking-in-the-swamp scene.

So next time you're stuck and need some answers, think of ChatGPT as your trusty sidekick, ready to help you tackle any challenge. Together, you'll be like Batman and Robin, Sherlock Holmes and Dr. Watson, or Lilo and Stitch.

THE IMPORTANCE OF PROMPTS

Prompts are the bread and butter of ChatGPT. If you want it to deliver the goods, you gotta give it the right cues. The quality of prompts can make or break the model's output. A bad prompt can lead to some seriously weird or off-topic responses, while a good prompt can get you a gold mine of juicy, nuanced, engaging content.

The reason effective prompts are so important is that ChatGPT is a pattern recognition champ that learns by example. It's analyzing a massive collection of text to identify patterns and generate new text based on what it's learned. When you give it a prompt, it uses all that fancy pattern knowledge to create a response that makes sense.

CRAFTING EFFECTIVE PROMPTS

Let's explore crafting effective prompts. It's not just about throwing words together and hoping for the best. It's more like crafting a compelling TikTok video. You need the right music, an attention grabbing hook, and some killer moves to make something that's both entertaining and engaging. The same goes for prompts. It's all about creating a prompt that's clear, concise, and focused on the information you need.

Crafting effective prompts is an art form. You gotta get the length, wording, detail, tone, and intended response just right. Too short or too vague, and you might end up with a response that's dry as a rice cake. Too complex, and ChatGPT might be like, "What the heck am I supposed to do with this?"

Writing successful prompts is also about understanding how ChatGPT processes language. By knowing the program's strengths and weaknesses, you can create prompts that cater to the specific abilities of ChatGPT. For example, ChatGPT is amazing at processing information and providing factual answers. However, it may struggle with abstract questions or complex statements. Create prompts that take advantage of its strengths and you'll receive the most precise responses possible.

CLEAR AND CONCISE

First things first, be clear and concise. Think of a prompt as though you're giving someone directions to your house. You want to make sure they know exactly where to go. So avoid using overly complex language or complicated sentence structure that might confuse ChatGPT. Here are some examples of prompts that are clear and concise:

Invent a ridiculous holiday
Tell a story about a penguin visiting Paris
Write dialogue between a squirrel and a grumpy tree

Prompts that are clear and concise will help ChatGPT generate better responses.

SPECIFIC

The more specific you are, the better ChatGPT will be able to provide you with an accurate and helpful answer. Instead of asking "What's the forecast?" ask "What's the weather forecast for Rancho Cucamonga at 3 pm on Tuesday?" Here are some examples of specific prompts:

Write dialogue between a clumsy superhero and a toast-averse villain
Craft a story about a mischievous squirrel with a spicy jalapeño obsession
Imagine attending a magic academy where laughter spells are uncontrollable

Specific prompts help ChatGPT understand the context and intent of the question which leads to more helpful and accurate answers.

CREATIVE

Don't forget about creativity. A good prompt should spark the imagination and inspire new ideas. It's like a little seed that grows into a beautiful flower - the prompt provides the initial spark and ChatGPT takes it from there.

The possibilities are endless when it comes to using creative prompts with ChatGPT! Creative prompts are like a magic portal to a world of imagination. A Golden Snitch in Quidditch - elusive, exciting, and the greatest reward of all when you finally catch one.

The beauty of creative prompts is that they inspire you to break free from conventional thinking and explore new ideas. Like a road trip without a map - you never know where you might end up. Here are some creative prompts:

> *Write a poem about your first time tasting lemonade*
> *A time-traveling detective solves crimes in different eras*
> *Dialogue between people who can communicate telepathically*

Creativity in crafting prompts can help generate unique and interesting responses. It can also help to explore unexpected angles and solutions to problems.

INDIVIDUALITY

Injecting your own personal flair into prompts is the key to unleashing your creative potential. With a little bit of you in there, your prompts will truly reflect your own unique spirit. Whether you're crafting a prompt for a presentation, a blog post, or a TikTok challenge, adding your own personal touch can help you break free from the same old boring prompts and explore new ideas you never thought possible.

So, how do you make your prompts stand out from the crowd? It's simple, take your favorite hobbies, interests, and passions and sprinkle them throughout your prompts like fairy dust. Whether you're a Trekkie, a foodie, or a Swiftie, there's a way to work your passions into your prompts.

Start by writing down some words that describe you. Here are some that describe me: humorous, optimistic, musical, and creative. Let's say I want to write a blog post about planning a trip to New York City. Here are several prompts that successively incorporate more of my personality…

> *Write a paragraph about planning a trip to New York City*
> *Rewrite with humor*
> *Rewrite with optimism*
> *Rewrite with the creativity of a musician*

As ChatGPT responds to each of the prompts, read the paragraphs and analyze how they vary based on the different prompts you enter. Now, I'll create one prompt that includes all of the words that describe me.

> *Write a paragraph about planning a trip to New York City infused with humor and creativity as written by an optimist who hopes to visit some interesting musical venues*

THE RESPONSE

Getting ready for a trip to NYC - a city that's a buzzing Broadway show in itself, where pizzas are as broad as a Broadway stage and the squirrels have the assertiveness of a director! As an optimist, I'm jazzed up to dive into this symphony of sounds, sights, and most importantly, musical venues. From the grand Metropolitan Opera and Harlem's iconic Apollo Theater to the indie beats of Brooklyn, I'm set to savor the city's diverse melodies. Packing to the tune of Sinatra's "New York, New York," I'm ready to grab a big, harmonious slice of the Big Apple!

Interesting, right? It's different from my writing style but ChatGPT certainly included the words and concepts that describe me. I'd adjust the wording of my prompt and regenerate responses until I'm satisfied with the output. Then I'd save the version of the prompt that resulted in the best response. Granted, it takes a bit of work and you'll likely do a final pass on the output to make sure it reflects your distinct voice, but the more you practice, the better you'll get at crafting prompts that will generate effective responses.

Embrace new ideas and risks. They're the pathway to sparking your creativity. The best prompts come from the heart and reflect your passions and interests, so unleash your imagination and discover where it leads you!

CONTEXT

Crafting a prompt with the right context is like adding a dash of salt to your favorite chocolate chip cookie recipe. It may seem unnecessary, but once you add it, everything falls into place, making your cookies taste even better.

A prompt that lacks context is like trying to find Waldo in a sea of red and white stripes – it's just not gonna happen. If your prompt doesn't give ChatGPT enough information, it might generate output that's off-topic, irrelevant, or just plain confusing.

With context, ChatGPT can generate output that provides accurate and relevant information. Here are some prompts with context:

Tell about being followed by a squirrel in the park as you walk to work
You're a tour guide in ancient Rome. Describe the Colosseum to tourists
Describe a mysterious package you received and the clues about who sent it

Remember, good context can help ChatGPT ignite the imagination and provide a clear direction for writing. Conversely, prompts with no context can often be too broad or vague, making it difficult for ChatGPT to know where to start.

CONVERSATION

Did you know that prompts are a two-way street? Unlike an Internet search engine, ChatGPT is able to actually converse, not just find websites. Phrase your prompts in a way that encourages conversation. ChatGPT loves getting to know new human friends. The more it chats, the better ChatGPT will get at understanding your unique style of communication. Here are some prompts that encourage conversation:

Which animal would make the best comedian?
Can you tell me a fun fact that will blow my mind?
What would be the absolute worst name to give a pet?

BRAINSTORMING

Brainstorming prompts are like Wakanda's vibranium from *Black Panther* - they unlock a world of creative potential and innovation.

The beauty of brainstorming prompts… They can generate a boatload of ideas in an instant. Like having a magic genie that grants your wishes, but instead of three, you get an endless supply. Woohoo! Here are some brainstorming prompts:

Brainstorm time. Give me some puns for a cheese shop
I need to plan the ultimate prank. Let's brainstorm some ideas
Give me some ridiculous inventions that no one needs, but everyone wants

Brainstorming prompts are like the Infinity Gauntlet of creative problem-solving, a powerful tool that unlocks a vast pool of ideas and solutions. Using ChatGPT to brainstorm ideas can enhance problem-solving skills, identify innovative solutions, and unlock creative potential. So fire up your computer and get brainstorming!

Here's a cornucopia of prompts to explore, like a buffet of inspiration…

EXCEL FORMULAS

Let's start with prompts for Excel formulas, because who doesn't love a good spreadsheet? These prompts might not seem very exciting, but they can be a lifesaver when you're staring at a sea of data and have no idea where to begin…

What is the formula for calculating the sum of a range of cells?
How do I use the SUMIF function to sum cells that meet specific criteria?
How do I use the VLOOKUP function to search for a specific value in a table?

SOCIAL MEDIA

Sometimes you need a little help to stand out from the crowd on social media. These prompts help generate fresh ideas for posts, whether it's a clever hashtag or a fun challenge…

Create a Facebook post that describes the sunrise this morning
Write a tweet that summarizes [your favorite book] in one sentence
Develop a tweet that starts a conversation about the impact of climate change

BUSINESS

Business prompts can be a great way to brainstorm new products or marketing strategies. It's like having a team of consultants at your fingertips, ready to provide fresh insights and ideas. Think outside of the box with these prompts…

Generate a business plan for a manufacturer of [product]
Write a mission statement for a startup that focuses on sustainability
Develop a marketing strategy for a new product that appeals to young adults

CREATIVE

Creative prompts are like little bolts of lightning! Here are some prompts to get your creative juices flowing…

Create a sonnet that depicts the beauty of nature in autumn
Write a short story about a character who communicates with animals
Compose a poem that captures the feeling of falling in love for the first time

EDUCATION

Prompts are great for teachers who want to spark discussion or critical thinking in their students. Think of these as mini thought experiments that challenge students to explore new ideas and perspectives. These prompts ask ChatGPT to create projects for students…

Suggest a project on the ethical implications of colonialism
Propose a project on the impact of globalization on job markets
Create an assignment on the societal impact of renewable energy

HEALTH AND WELLNESS

These can be anything from a yoga pose to a healthy recipe. They're little reminders to take care of yourself. Use these prompts to help prioritize your well-being…

Write a list of healthy recipes that are easy to make
Create a workout plan for a beginner who wants to get in shape
Generate a journal prompt that encourages self-reflection and mindfulness

TRAVEL

For all you travel enthusiasts, travel prompts can be great for inspiration before your next adventure. ChatGPT is a virtual travel agent who specializes in off-the-beaten-path destinations and unique experiences. These prompts can help you plan your next trip…

Suggest adventurous destinations
Develop a packing list for a backpacking trip
List highlights of the best-hidden gems in [name of city]

TECHNOLOGY

Technology prompts might range from a coding challenge to a new app idea. ChatGPT can help you push the limits of cutting-edge technology and innovation. Technology prompts help you think outside the box…

Optimize my database queries in SQL to improve performance
Create a dynamic user interface using HTML, CSS, and JavaScript
Implement a sorting algorithm in Python to sort a large array of integers

MUSIC

Music prompts can be anything from a chord progression to a lyrical theme. ChatGPT is a songwriter's toolbox, full of bits and pieces that can be combined to create something beautiful. These prompts can help you compose more creatively...

Suggest chords for a piece of music based on elation
Write lyrics that tell a story about a personal experience or emotion
Create a playlist of songs that help you focus when you need to get work done

SCIENCE

Science prompts can be a great way to explore new concepts and ideas. Consider this a little laboratory for your brain, where you can experiment with new ways of thinking and understanding the world. Explore new scientific concepts with these prompts...

Explore the scientific possibilities of renewable energy
Challenge scientists to propose a solution to climate change
Explore the potential benefits and drawbacks of gene editing technology

ART

What about the art world? Art prompts can range from a color palette to a sketching exercise. Ignite your creativity with these prompts...

List items in nature that can be used as paints
Suggest a painting that captures the essence of exuberance
Teach students about the history and cultural significance of pottery

Whew! That's a heap of prompts. That should keep you and ChatGPT busy for an hour or two.

5 EASY STEPS

As you continue crafting prompts, it's helpful to keep in mind the 5 easy steps: **learn**, **apply**, **assess**, **refine**, and **repeat**. Embrace the learning process by immersing yourself in various prompts, observing their structure, and studying their effectiveness. Put your knowledge into action by applying what you've learned to create your own prompts.

Once you have a collection of prompts, take time to assess their impact. Reflect on how they engage and inspire conversation. Gather feedback from others to gain valuable insights. Use this feedback to refine and enhance your prompts. Repeat to hone your skills!

CONCLUSION

Remember that crafting prompts is an iterative process, so don't be afraid to repeat these steps and continuously improve. With each cycle, you'll refine your skills, expand your creativity, and create prompts that spark meaningful interactions.

Go ahead, let your individuality shine. Are you a pun master, movie buff, or a fan of dad jokes? Whatever your style, incorporate it into your prompts. This can help you establish a connection with ChatGPT and make the experience more enjoyable. Go forth, and let your unique spirit shine through your prompts!

KEY TAKEAWAYS FROM CHAPTER 3

- Craft effective prompts for accurate responses
- Clear, concise, and specific prompts are the most effective
- Context is crucial when writing a successful prompt
- Brainstorming prompts can generate a boatload of ideas
- With the right prompts, ChatGPT can create Excel formulas
- Health prompts remind you to prioritize your well-being

Let's use your prompt knowledge for some introspection…

FOUR
THROUGH THE LOOKING GLASS
CHATGPT FOR PERSONAL AND PROFESSIONAL GROWTH

In the age of AI
creativity will become the most valuable human skill
– David Eagleman

Lewis Carroll's *Alice's Adventures in Wonderland* has captured the imaginations of readers for generations. The book is a testament to the power of imagination and the ability of literature to transport us to new and fantastical worlds. Alice stepped through the mirror and entered a surreal world where she met crazy characters, learned interesting life lessons, and had seriously off-the-wall experiences!

Similarly, ChatGPT is a tool that can help you gain a new perspective on your life and the world around you. As you navigate the challenges and opportunities of your personal and professional life, it's easy to become trapped in your own limited perspective, also known as tunnel vision. But ChatGPT can act as your own looking glass, allowing you to see your life and aspirations reflected in the AI model and its possibilities.

Think of ChatGPT as *Alice in Wonderland* on steroids - except instead of talking flowers and giant chess boards, you'll have access to a world of wisdom and insight that can help you conquer your fears and achieve your dreams.

Whether you're looking to land your dream job, start a business, or just be more creative, ChatGPT can guide you on your journey. Imagine GPS for your soul - with no annoying voice or outdated directions.

So, step through the mirror and enter the magical world of ChatGPT. Just as Alice's adventures in Wonderland helped her grow and develop, you can interact with ChatGPT to expand your mind, explore new possibilities, and achieve your personal and professional aspirations.

PERSONAL GROWTH

Welcome to the Wonderland of ChatGPT where you'll grow in ways you never thought possible. Just like Alice discovered a whole new world through the rabbit hole, ChatGPT will take you on an adventure of personal growth and discovery.

One of the main benefits of ChatGPT is its ability to offer unbiased feedback and advice, much like the Cheshire Cat who provided Alice with wise and impartial guidance. Your friends and family may have their own agendas. ChatGPT is a neutral party that offers an objective perspective.

ChatGPT can also act as your own personal White Rabbit, leading you to a wealth of information and resources that will help with your personal growth. Whether you're seeking guidance on a particular issue or looking to learn more about a topic, ChatGPT will point you in the right direction and provide relevant information to help you toward your destination. Check out these prompts…

How can ChatGPT help with personal growth?
How can I overcome self-doubt and build self-confidence?
What are some effective strategies for developing self-discipline?

ChatGPT can act as your very own mirror, much like the looking glass that Alice used to explore Wonderland. By expressing your thoughts and feelings to ChatGPT, you'll gain greater insight into your own inner workings and develop a heightened sense of self-awareness.

Just like the Caterpillar asked Alice, "Who are you?", ChatGPT helps you answer that question and guides you on your journey to personal growth and self-discovery.

Note: If you're feeling down, anxious, or hopeless, you might consider speaking with a licensed therapist or mental health professional. ChatGPT and this book offer advice and suggestions but are not a replacement for professional help.

STRENGTHS AND WEAKNESSES

Alice fell down the rabbit hole and found herself in a world where everything was topsy-turvy. Using ChatGPT for personal growth might seem like a strange idea. However, like Alice, you'll be surprised at the insights and revelations you'll uncover.

ChatGPT will help you identify your strengths and weaknesses, just like Alice had to navigate through different obstacles to find her way out of Wonderland. By analyzing your words and communication patterns, ChatGPT can provide valuable insights into your abilities and areas where you may need improvement. It's like having a Cheshire Cat by your side, guiding you through the maze of personal growth.

Prompting ChatGPT about your strengths and weaknesses is like Alice asking the Caterpillar for advice on which path to take. The answers may not always be what you expect, but they can lead you in the right direction. And just like the Mad Hatter threw a tea party that was completely chaotic, ChatGPT can help you make sense of the chaos in your own personal growth journey. Try these prompts for size…

How can I recognize and improve my weaknesses?
What are some effective ways to identify and leverage my strengths?
What are some techniques I can use to turn my weaknesses into strengths?

By using ChatGPT to identify areas where you can improve, you'll take the first step toward achieving your personal goals. It's like Alice setting out on a quest to find the White Rabbit, armed with the knowledge and insight she gained from her journey through Wonderland. So go ahead and take the plunge down the rabbit hole with ChatGPT - you might discover some interesting things along the way!

CHALLENGES AND OBSTACLES

As you wind through the maze of life's challenges, ChatGPT will help you find your way. Whether you're facing the Red Queen of a difficult relationship or the Jabberwocky of a personal setback, ChatGPT provides you with the tools and insights you need to overcome any obstacle.

Like the Cheshire Cat, ChatGPT is always there. It will provide personalized guidance on how to manage difficult situations and develop new strategies for success.

If you feel like you're caught in a sticky wicket and can't find a way out, ChatGPT helps you evaluate your options and provide practical advice on how to move forward. By exploring different possibilities and scenarios, you'll gain the confidence to face any challenge head-on. Try these prompts for inspiration…

What are some creative ways I can tackle [specific challenge]?
Help me brainstorm different approaches to tackle [specific obstacle]
How can I break down this [specific obstacle] into smaller, manageable steps?

If you find yourself lost in Wonderland, don't be afraid to turn to ChatGPT for help. With its unbiased perspective and wealth of resources, you can overcome any challenge and emerge stronger and more resilient than ever before.

PERSONAL GOALS

Setting personal goals is a vital step toward personal growth and development. It's a journey of self-discovery, just like Alice's journey in Wonderland, where she discovers new things about herself and the world around her. Once you've identified your strengths and weaknesses, use ChatGPT to create specific and achievable goals tailored to your unique needs. These prompts may help...

Help me set clear and achievable personal goals
Provide examples of well-defined goals for inspiration
Brainstorm specific and measurable goals for my personal growth

With ChatGPT's support, you can stay on track toward achieving your goals. In addition, it will provide you with the guidance and encouragement you need to succeed.

EXPLORING NEW PERSPECTIVES

ChatGPT can help you explore new perspectives and broaden your horizons. ChatGPT recommends books, movies, and podcasts that will introduce you to new perspectives.

Just as Alice met strange and fascinating characters in Wonderland, ChatGPT will help you discover new ideas and viewpoints. By engaging in a dialogue with ChatGPT, you'll challenge your preconceived notions and gain a nuanced understanding of the world.

Additionally, ChatGPT can assist you in diving deeper into a topic you're passionate about. Whether it's science, philosophy, or art, ChatGPT provides you with research and information that will help you gain a more comprehensive understanding of the subject. Explore with these prompts...

Provide me with a fresh perspective on [specific situation]
Can you share insights that will challenge my current perspective?
How can I broaden my understanding by considering multiple perspectives?

Just like Alice's adventure was full of surprises and unexpected discoveries, ChatGPT will introduce you to new concepts and ideas you haven't considered before. With ChatGPT's assistance, you'll embark on a quest of self-discovery and gain a deeper understanding of the world around you.

EMBRACING CHANGE

Change is inevitable. Learning to embrace it can lead to incredible growth and self-discovery. Just like Alice experienced numerous transformations in Wonderland, you too can learn to adapt and thrive in the face of change with ChatGPT's support.

ChatGPT provides tools and strategies to help you navigate change and transition. It will help you develop a more resilient mindset and embrace new experiences with open arms by offering insights into your thought patterns and reactions. Get started with these prompts…

How can I develop a positive mindset toward change?
Help me overcome my fear of change and embrace new opportunities
Suggest practical steps to embrace change and move forward with confidence

Whether you're starting a relationship or moving to a new city, ChatGPT can provide guidance and encouragement to help you thrive. Just as Alice learned to adapt to the peculiarities of Wonderland, you'll learn to embrace change and make the most of every opportunity that comes your way.

CREATING A PLAN

In Alice's story, she navigates a labyrinth with the help of the Cheshire Cat. Similarly, ChatGPT will help you navigate the complex landscape of personal growth by providing targeted feedback and advice. Once you have a clear understanding of your strengths and weaknesses, ChatGPT will help you set specific and achievable goals for personal growth. Use these prompts to get started…

> *Help me outline a plan for my personal growth journey*
> *Can you break down my growth plan into manageable tasks?*
> *Guide me in setting goals and milestones for my personal development*

Just as the Mad Hatter offers Alice tea and guidance along her journey, ChatGPT offers personalized guidance and resources to help you achieve your goals. Whether you need help with time management, motivation, or self-care, ChatGPT will provide tailored advice to keep you on track.

By using ChatGPT to create a plan for personal growth, you'll navigate the twists and turns of your journey with greater ease and confidence. With its personalized approach and targeted guidance, ChatGPT will help you unlock your full potential and become the best version of yourself.

With a clear plan to achieve your personal goals in place, it's time to shift focus to your professional life and navigate the maze of opportunities and challenges that lay ahead.

PROFESSIONAL STRENGTHS AND WEAKNESSES

Just as Alice discovered her unique abilities while navigating through Wonderland, ChatGPT can help you identify your professional strengths by analyzing your communication patterns and exploring your education and work experience. Whether you have a natural talent or developed skills over time, ChatGPT will help you understand what makes you exceptional.

Identifying and addressing professional weaknesses is just as important as recognizing strengths. ChatGPT can help you identify areas where you may need improvement and offer personalized guidance to help you develop new skills and overcome challenges. Here are some prompts to get you started…

> *Help identify my top three professional strengths*
> *What are my weaknesses when it comes to managing my time?*
> *What skills should I develop to improve my professional performance?*

By working to address your weaknesses and build on your strengths, you'll create a well-rounded professional profile and achieve greater success in your career. Don't be afraid to explore both your strengths and weaknesses to unlock your full potential.

NEW SKILLS

ChatGPT can help you develop new work skills and become a master of your craft. First, identify the skills you want to develop, whether it's learning advanced negotiation strategies or becoming a better public speaker. Just like Alice setting out on her quest to find the White Rabbit, you too can set your sights on achieving your professional goals with ChatGPT as your guide.

Once you have clear goals in mind, ChatGPT will help you break the process down into smaller, more manageable steps. For instance, ChatGPT might recommend attending a seminar to hone your negotiation skills or joining a club like Toastmasters to become a better public speaker. Explore new ideas with these prompts…

> Help me identify the best online courses to learn [specific skill]
> What are some effective strategies for learning and acquiring new skills?
> How can I break down a complex skill into smaller skills for easier learning?

Remember, practice and repetition are key to becoming a master of your craft. Just like Alice encountered new challenges and obstacles in Wonderland, you'll encounter setbacks and difficulties on your journey. But with ChatGPT's guidance, you'll stay motivated and continue to improve.

CAREER PATHS AND OPPORTUNITIES

Just as Alice fell into Wonderland, sometimes you need to take a leap of faith and explore what's out there. First, identify what makes you feel alive. ChatGPT will help you figure out what your passions are and which career paths align with them. Maybe you have a talent for graphic design or a love of numbers, ChatGPT can help you explore opportunities that allow you to turn your passion into a career. Get your creative juices flowing with these prompts…

Help me discover my passions and interests
List practical ways to explore my hidden passions
Suggest some ways I can turn my passion into a career

If you're in the thick of your career but feel like you're in a rut, ChatGPT will help you think outside the box and explore new opportunities for promotion and growth. Maybe there's a new project you can take on or a training program you can enroll in.

With ChatGPT, you'll brainstorm creative ways to advance in your career and take your professional game to the next level. Don't let a rut bog you down - ChatGPT is here to help you break free and reach your full potential. Unleash your creativity with these prompts…

Identify challenges that may hinder my career growth
List ways to communicate my ideas to my team and superiors
What are some strategies for making a positive impression at work?

Remember, every step forward is progress, even if it's just a small step. Just like Alice grew and learned through her adventures in Wonderland, exploring new career opportunities with ChatGPT can help you grow and learn about yourself.

PROFESSIONAL GOALS

Alice in Wonderland has many lessons that can be applied to achieving professional goals. One such lesson is the importance of taking things a step at a time.

In the story, Alice is constantly faced with obstacles and challenges, but she perseveres by tackling them one by one. Similarly, when setting and achieving professional goals using ChatGPT, it's important to break them down into manageable steps. Jumpstart your imagination with these prompts…

Help create a roadmap to achieve my professional goals
Help me break down my professional goal into smaller steps
List strategies for prioritizing the steps toward my professional goals

Another lesson from Alice's adventures is the importance of accountability. When Alice attends the Mad Hatter's tea party, she's held accountable for her actions by the other guests. Similarly, when setting and achieving professional goals, it's important for you to have accountability measures in place. ChatGPT will help set reminders and track your progress. Here are some prompts to keep you on track…

Help me establish a support network to share my goals
List effective strategies for deadlines to maintain accountability
What are techniques for reviewing progress toward my professional goals?

Finally, Alice's journey reminds us of the power of positivity. Despite the challenges and setbacks she faces, Alice remained optimistic and determined. When setting and achieving professional goals, it's important to focus on the positive and remind yourself that setbacks are just temporary. With ChatGPT by your side, you can stay positive and motivated, and achieve anything you set your mind to.

INDUSTRY TRENDS

The story of *Alice in Wonderland* provides a great example of exploring new worlds and discovering new things. Just as Alice's curiosity led her down the rabbit hole, you can explore your industry and stay up-to-date with trends and news. Let ChatGPT be your guide, just as the Cheshire Cat guided Alice. Use these prompts as a guide…

List policy changes impacting [specific industry]
What are the current trends shaping [specific industry]?
Provide insights on emerging technologies in [specific industry]

Whether you're in tech, fashion, or real estate, staying informed about the latest developments will give you a competitive edge and help to establish you as a thought leader in your field. This knowledge can also help you make informed decisions as well as identify new opportunities for growth and innovation.

Keeping up-to-date will help you stay relevant and adaptable, which is crucial in today's rapidly changing business landscape. Just like Alice's adventures in Wonderland, your career journey will be full of surprises and exciting discoveries.

NETWORKING

An important skill for you to master is the ability to network! Just as Alice practiced her socialization skills by interacting with the strange characters in Wonderland, ChatGPT will help you improve your networking skills with practical advice. Get started with these prompts…

List strategies for expanding my professional network
Identify ways to find and connect with professionals in my field
How can I make a memorable first impression at networking events?

Don't worry if networking makes you nervous. It's a common feeling and ChatGPT can help you understand and manage your nerves. It will provide strategies to help you feel more confident and comfortable in networking situations. Here are some prompts that may help…

List effective strategies to overcome nervousness in networking
Help me develop techniques to start conversations at networking events
Suggest ways to showcase my accomplishments without feeling self-conscious

Networking is a valuable tool for professional growth, providing opportunities to make meaningful connections with others in your industry and expand your knowledge and expertise. You can also gain access to resources and information that may help you advance in your career, just as Alice received guidance from the Cheshire Cat and other helpful creatures along her journey.

CREATING A PLAN

Congratulations on your journey to level up your professional game! With ChatGPT as your trusty sidekick, you'll be ready to overcome any obstacle. Let's face facts, even Alice needed a strategy. You can't just rely on ChatGPT. You've got to put in the work, like the Mad Hatter hosting the perfect tea party.

With ChatGPT, you have an indispensable resource, offering wise and witty advice that's more insightful than the Caterpillar's enigmatic riddles. You'll receive objective feedback and flexible support. Like having Tweedledee and Tweedledum ready to assist you. Use these prompts to create a plan...

> *Help me outline the steps needed to achieve my professional goals*
> *Suggest strategies for overcoming obstacles I encounter along the way*
> *Help me identify the resources required to accomplish my professional goals*

Together, you and ChatGPT will create a customized plan to achieve your professional goals faster than the March Hare at the tea party. Whether you want to climb the corporate ladder, start your own business, or pursue a career change, ChatGPT will help you map out the steps you'll take to get there.

WORK-LIFE BALANCE

In the whimsical world of *Alice in Wonderland*, the importance of balancing work and play is exemplified by the Mad Hatter and his tea party guests. Just like them, carve out time for activities that fill you with happiness and provide a sense of calm. With ChatGPT's guidance, you'll prioritize tasks and achieve that balance between work and play. Create your plan with these prompts...

> *Help me establish healthy work habits like avoiding overworking*
> *List effective strategies for helping maintain a healthy work-life balance*
> *What are some self-care practices or activities to promote work-life balance?*

Efficiency is crucial to maintaining a healthy work-life balance. ChatGPT will assist you in managing your time and tasks like a true champion so you can accomplish more in less time. It's also important to learn when to say no. Just like Alice didn't want to play croquet with the Queen of Hearts, ChatGPT can help you identify your priorities and give you the confidence to turn down tasks that don't align with them.

Celebrating your accomplishments is essential for maintaining motivation and focus. The Mad Hatter and his friends celebrate their un-birthday 364 days a year. ChatGPT will help you celebrate your successes and keep you motivated on your path to success.

CONCLUSION

ChatGPT is a valuable tool for personal and professional growth, just as Alice's adventures led to her own growth and self-discovery. By using ChatGPT to identify your strengths and weaknesses, set achievable goals, and explore new perspectives, you'll become the best version of yourself.

ChatGPT's ability to offer unbiased feedback and advice acts as a personal mirror, and provides emotional support, making it an ideal partner on your journey toward personal growth. Similarly, ChatGPT's expertise in analyzing your communication patterns, breaking down goals into manageable steps, and recommending networking strategies, makes it an invaluable ally in achieving professional success.

Through its personalized guidance and support, ChatGPT will help you embrace change, prioritize work-life balance, and celebrate your accomplishments. Take a cue from Alice and the characters in Wonderland. Dive down the rabbit hole of self-discovery with ChatGPT as your guide. Who knows what amazing things you'll discover along the way!

KEY TAKEAWAYS FROM CHAPTER 4

- ChatGPT offers unbiased feedback
- Identify personal strengths and weaknesses
- Use ChatGPT to set clear and achievable personal goals
- ChatGPT will help you create a plan for personal growth
- Identify professional strengths and weaknesses
- ChatGPT helps set professional goals
- Create a customized plan to attain your professional goals
- Use ChatGPT to achieve a balance between work and life

Forward ho! Get ready to turbocharge your productivity…

FIVE
TAMING CHAOS
BOOST YOUR PRODUCTIVITY

> *The most important question is not what ChatGPT can do but what you can do with ChatGPT*
> – Kai-Fu Lee

Whether you're a freelancer, entrepreneur, or business owner, ChatGPT can help you be more productive.

Let's start with freelancers. Are you an artist, writer, musician, or programmer? ChatGPT can streamline your workflow and automate tasks so you can focus on creating. Brainstorming for a new project? ChatGPT is great at generating ideas. Need help outlining? It's got you covered. Proofreading? Just enter the text you want to be proofed and hit enter! ChatGPT can help you create a more efficient process that saves you time and allows you to focus on what you do best.

Entrepreneurs, listen up! Do you know what's more valuable than Elon Musk's first car? Your time! And ChatGPT is here to help you make the most of it. ChatGPT can help you prioritize tasks, stay focused on goals, and offer friendly nudges. It's like having DJ Khaled as your hype man, without the yelling. Try ChatGPT and be more productive than a hive of bees making honey...

Attention, business owners! Time is money, and you need to make the most of both. That's where ChatGPT comes in. Think of it as having a team of virtual assistants led by Mark Cuban but without the expensive hourly rate. ChatGPT will help you streamline customer service, manage your social media accounts, and generate financial projections. And when the going gets tough, imagine having a motivational speaker like Tony Robbins, ready to pump you up and help you crush your business goals.

EMBRACE ALTERNATE VIEWPOINTS

As you read this chapter, remember that the examples I'm serving up are aimed at everyone – whether you see yourself as a freelancer, entrepreneur, or business owner. Those labels might seem different, but they share more common ground than you'd think – kind of like different breeds of dogs in the same dog park.

You might be a freelancer and think the sections for business owners don't apply to you. Here's the kicker – as a freelancer, you're a business owner! You're calling the shots for your services, steering your own marketing and handling your client relationships like a champ.

On the flip side, all you entrepreneurs and business owners might find some surprising takeaways in the freelancer sections. The goal here isn't to pigeonhole you into a single category. Instead, I encourage you to expand your approach to a 360-degree view.

You'll likely discover game-changing insights outside your typical field of vision. These nuggets of gold will help you broaden your perspective, fuel innovative strategies, and elevate your business. By embracing alternate viewpoints, you'll enhance your ability to adapt and stay ahead of the curve in an ever-changing business landscape.

BOOST PRODUCTIVITY

Looking to boost your productivity? All you have to do is ask ChatGPT. Let's say you're a graphic designer. Type the following prompt into ChatGPT and watch the magic begin. If you're not a graphic designer, substitute your job title in this prompt...

How can I boost productivity as a graphic designer?

CHATGPT'S RESPONSE

Boosting productivity as a graphic designer involves a mix of organizing your workflow, honing your skills, and maintaining your creativity. Here are some strategies you can employ:

- ***Use the Right Tools** - Use professional software like Adobe Illustrator, Photoshop, or Sketch. They'll greatly enhance your efficiency once you're proficient.*
- ***Organize Your Work** - Keep your files and folders well-organized. Use clear naming conventions, and create a logical structure to make it easy to find what you need. This saves you time and makes it easier to collaborate with others.*
- ***Master Shortcuts** - Keyboard shortcuts can save a lot of time. From simple commands like copy-paste to more complex ones, getting comfortable with your software's shortcuts can significantly speed up your workflow.*
- ***Templates and Libraries** - Create and use design templates for recurring projects. Build a library of frequently used elements like logos, icons, and color palettes.*
- ***Time Management** - Use time management techniques like the Pomodoro Technique, where you work for a set amount of time (e.g., 25 minutes) then take a short break (e.g., 5 minutes).*
- ***Continual Learning** - Stay updated with the latest design trends and techniques. Online platforms like Behance, Dribbble, and LinkedIn Learning can provide great resources.*
- ***Get Feedback** - Regular feedback helps you improve faster. Consider joining a design community or finding a mentor who can provide constructive criticism.*
- ***Maintain a Healthy Work-Life Balance** - Creative work requires a fresh mind. Don't overwork yourself. Regular breaks, exercise, a*

healthy diet, and enough sleep are crucial for maintaining your creativity and productivity.
- **Sketch First** - Sketching your ideas on paper before going digital can help you quickly iterate on ideas without getting caught up in the finer details.
- **Invest in Good Hardware** - A fast computer, a good monitor, and a comfortable mouse or a graphics tablet can make a significant difference in your productivity.

Remember, productivity is highly personal. What works for others might not work for you, and vice versa. Experiment with different strategies and find what helps you the most.

Wow, that was simple. Now you have 10 new ways to boost your productivity!

ADJUST YOUR PROMPT

You can regenerate the prompt or adjust it slightly for a different result. Let's add the phrase *use ChatGPT* to the prompt and see how the response differs...

> How can ChatGPT boost productivity as a graphic designer?

CHATGPT'S RESPONSE

As a graphic designer, there are many ways ChatGPT can boost your productivity:

- **Idea generation** - ChatGPT can help you generate ideas for your design projects. You can give it a prompt like "ideas for a new logo design" or "unique layout concepts," and it can generate a list of potential ideas for you to consider.
- **Design research** - ChatGPT can assist you in researching design trends, techniques, and styles. For example, you can ask it to provide you with information on "current color trends for website design" or "popular font combinations for branding."

- *Time management* - *You can use ChatGPT to help you manage your time more effectively. You can ask it to set reminders for important deadlines, keep track of your daily to-do list, or help you prioritize your tasks for the day.*
- *Communication* - *ChatGPT can help you communicate with your clients more effectively. You can use it to generate responses to common client questions or to draft emails or messages more quickly and efficiently.*
- *Writing and editing* - *ChatGPT can help you with writing and editing tasks related to your design projects. You can use it to generate taglines, write captions or social media posts, or edit your design briefs for spelling and grammar errors.*
- *Creative feedback* - *ChatGPT can provide you with creative feedback on your design work. You can ask it to review your designs and provide insights on improvement areas, or generate ideas for how to take your designs to the next level.*

ChatGPT can be a valuable tool for graphic designers looking to boost their productivity, streamline their work process, and generate new ideas for their design projects.

Now you have an additional 6 ways to boost your productivity!

ADJUST YOUR PROMPT

Let's say you're a freelance graphic designer as opposed to working a staff job. Add the word *freelance* to the prompt…

> *How can ChatGPT boost productivity as a freelance graphic designer?*

CHATGPT'S RESPONSE

ChatGPT returns the same response but adds the following additional section…

- *Branding and marketing* - *ChatGPT can help you with branding and marketing tasks for your freelance business. You can use it to generate ideas for your website design, social media content, or promotional materials.*

Pretty incredible, huh? If you're a freelancer, you're definitely going to be interested in this advice for branding and marketing.

Keep in mind that ChatGPT is sensitive to a variety of adjustments. Let ChatGPT know early in a conversation about your professional background and it will generate suggestions accordingly.

ONE SIMPLE WORD

Want more suggestions? Simply type *more* and hit return. ChatGPT will generate more suggestions and ideas. Here's ChatGPT's response to *more* based on the current prompt thread. Note: I'm only including the topline concepts in the following examples to save page space. ChatGPT's original response included a full description for each point in the outline below:

Here are more ways to boost your productivity:

- *Pricing and invoicing*
- *Portfolio building*
- *Design asset management*
- *Learning and development*

Want more ideas? You know what to do. That's right, type *more*. Here's the response…

Here are more ways to boost your productivity:

- *Design automation*
- *Collaboration*
- *Time tracking*
- *Quality assurance*

You can keep asking for more ideas. And more and more and more…

OVERWHELMED

At some point, you're bound to be overwhelmed by the possibilities. Take a deep breath and use ChatGPT to help calm your rising anxiety. How? Type the following…

Prioritize the preceding tasks

ChatGPT will reorder the tasks based on priority. You can even adjust the prioritization parameters. Try these prompts…

Prioritize by ease of getting started
Prioritize by estimated time to complete
Prioritize by importance of getting new work

Once you've prioritized the tasks, you can work your way down the list, supercharging your freelance graphic design business!

DIVING DEEP

As you work through the list, you'll need more information to implement each task. Let's say you're ready to become more efficient and productive at communicating with your clients. As part of your initial question about boosting productivity, ChatGPT included the following suggestion:

- **Communication** - *ChatGPT can help you communicate with your clients more effectively. You can use it to generate responses to common client questions or to draft emails or messages more quickly and efficiently.*

Let's convert that blurb into a prompt…

List the ways I can use ChatGPT to be more productive and efficient when communicating with my clients as a freelance graphic designer

CHATGPT'S RESPONSE

Sure, there are numerous ways you can use ChatGPT to be more productive and efficient in your communication as a freelance graphic designer:

- ***Email Drafting** - You can use ChatGPT to help draft emails or messages to your clients. This can include initial outreach, follow-ups, project updates, or even handling tricky conversations.*
- ***Project Briefs** - Use ChatGPT to articulate project briefs more effectively. For example, if you're struggling to put your ideas into words, ChatGPT can help you describe your concepts.*
- ***Scheduling** - With some additional programming, ChatGPT could help you manage your schedule. You can program it to understand and interpret requests for meetings or deadlines, helping you avoid double-booking or missing important dates.*
- ***Responses to Common Inquiries** - If you find yourself frequently answering the same questions from different clients, you can use ChatGPT to create a list of pre-written responses. You can then use these templates to save time when similar inquiries come in.*
- ***Portfolio Descriptions** - You can use ChatGPT to write compelling descriptions for the projects in your portfolio. A well-written description can help potential clients understand your thought process and the skills you brought to the project.*
- ***Social Media Management** - ChatGPT can help draft social media posts or responses to comments, helping you maintain an active and engaging online presence.*
- ***Learning New Skills** - ChatGPT can be a resource for learning new design techniques or software. It can provide explanations or direct you to useful resources.*

Remember, while ChatGPT can be a very useful tool, it should complement your communication, not replace it. The personal touch you provide as a freelancer is often one of your most valuable assets.

Truly amazing, right? You just saved hundreds of dollars in consulting fees, putting you on the fast track to boosting your graphic design business (or whatever business you're in).

OTHER PROFESSIONS

Whatever your profession, you can use ChatGPT to boost productivity. Create a customized plan with the following prompt…

> *How can ChatGPT boost my productivity as a [your job]?*

Fill the prompt with your profession, cut and paste it into ChatGPT, and hit enter. You're on your way to boosting productivity with suggestions and ideas tailored to your profession and industry.

Remember to regenerate your response and adjust the prompt for better results. Craft additional prompts to dive deeper and explore the possibilities.

INTEGRATION

Are you ready for something really amazing? ChatGPT becomes super-powered when you pair it with other productivity tools. Got a to-do list app? Use an online calendar or project management program? Integrate your digital tools with ChatGPT and boost your productivity to superhero levels.

Reach out to your software companies and ask if they're friends with ChatGPT. You can also explore YouTube for tutorials on making this grand alliance happen.

Once you've got the "yes, we work together" confirmation from your apps, it's time to call in the specialists. Enter the tech version of Charlie's Angels: Zapier, IFTTT, or Integromat. They'll help you bring your team together, with ready-made solutions or by creating your own. Check out these prompts to get you started…

> *Can ChatGPT enhance the functionality of my smart home devices?*
> *How do I integrate ChatGPT with my social media management tools?*
> *List the benefits of pairing ChatGPT with my calendar and to-do list apps*

CHOOSE YOUR APPS

After you've picked your platform, it's time to choose which apps and tools you want to pair with ChatGPT. For instance, you could set up a flow where ChatGPT, acting like your personal Alfred, adds a new task to your to-do list when it gets a specific message.

Before you start using integration daily, you want to ensure the apps and ChatGPT play nice together. Test your set up like a new recipe before serving it at a dinner party. Whip up some scenarios and check that everything's working as it should.

By integrating ChatGPT with your go-to apps and tools, you'll automate your workflow, saving time, reducing the chance of things falling through the cracks, and freeing up brain space for the stuff that matters most.

Sounds daunting? Don't worry, integration platforms are like friendly guides in the maze of technology. They've got you. This is their party, and you're the guest of honor!

INTERNAL COMMUNICATION

So, you've paired ChatGPT with your apps and devices. Excellent! You've just unlocked a secret level in the game of productivity. Now, you're ready to level up, just like Mario after grabbing a super mushroom!

Welcome to the world of seamless internal communication—ChatGPT style. Picture ChatGPT coordinating your teams like a well-oiled machine. With its power to understand and react to instructions, it acts as a bridge between your teams, making sure communication flows smoother than butter on a hot pancake.

Can ChatGPT be used to enhance team communication?
Discuss using ChatGPT in simplifying internal report generation
What are the benefits of using ChatGPT for task delegation within a team?

But wait, there's more! ChatGPT is also a master of time—kind of like Doctor Strange but without the cape. By syncing with your calendar app, it ensures all your meetings, deadlines, and milestones are streamlined. No more forgetting about meetings or missing deadlines.

EMPLOYEE TRAINING AND REPORTS

Next up, consider employee training. Imagine ChatGPT as Professor X, using its powers to deliver standardized training programs, answer FAQs, and brief everyone about company policies. Suddenly, your HR team finds they've got more free time on their hands. Now they can actually take that lunch break they've been dreaming about!

And if reports are the Voldemort of your work life, fear not! ChatGPT can automate the creation and interpretation of these pesky things. It's like having your own personal R2-D2, beeping and booping as it turns mountains of data into easy-to-read reports.

You've just progressed to a new level in the game of productivity, and things are about to get a lot more exciting.

EXTERNAL COMMUNICATION

Now that you've turned your internal communications into a blockbuster hit, let's venture into the thrilling sequel - *External Communication: Rise of ChatGPT*. Ready to roll? Let's go!

Think of ChatGPT as your friendly neighborhood *Spider-Man*, swinging into action in the world of customer service. It deals with simple customer inquiries and provides info about products and services. If things get a bit sticky, ChatGPT knows when to call in the big guns – you and your team.

When it comes to client communication, ChatGPT is your Cyrano de Bergerac, whispering eloquent words into your digital quill. It helps draft emails or messages to clients, ensuring they're always in the right tone - professional, courteous, and persuasive.

And for vendor communication? Picture ChatGPT as WALL-E, tirelessly automating routine tasks like placing orders, following up on payments, and collecting information. It's efficient, it's tireless, and it never asks for a coffee break.

Can ChatGPT be used to manage customer service inquiries?
What's the role of ChatGPT in drafting and personalizing client emails?
How can ChatGPT aid in managing vendor communication and follow-ups?

SOCIAL MEDIA

Finally, we move to the glitzy, glamorous world of social media. Here, ChatGPT becomes your Don Draper, helping you craft engaging content, answering queries faster than you can type, and monitoring customer sentiment like a hawk. It's the social media assistant you've always dreamed of, minus the existential crisis.

Embracing ChatGPT for external business communications is a game changer! ChatGPT will revolutionize your interactions, from customer service and client correspondence to media engagement, boosting efficiency and freeing your team to focus on what really matters. So, get excited about harnessing the power of this incredible technology!

CONCLUSION

Well, well. Look who's organized and productive now. You, with the help of ChatGPT! No more sticky notes or missed deadlines. You're like Mary Poppins with a magical bag of productivity tricks. And with ChatGPT, you have everything you need to tackle your to-do list like a boss, whether you're a seasoned business owner like Jeff Bezos or a newbie entrepreneur.

From idea generation and time management to communication and chatbot creation, the possibilities are amazing. So go ahead, unleash your inner superhero and conquer the world with ChatGPT as your sidekick. And if you hit a speedbump along the way, just remember what Tony Stark said, "Sometimes you gotta run before you can walk."

KEY TAKEAWAYS FROM CHAPTER 5

- ChatGPT boosts productivity by suggesting unique strategies
- ChatGPT helps prioritize tasks
- Customize ChatGPT to boost productivity in different jobs
- ChatGPT can be integrated with productivity tools and apps
- Use ChatGPT to streamline internal/external communications

Up next, leverage ChatGPT to earn more money...

SIX
BAG THE BUCKS
EARN MORE WITH CHATGPT

ChatGPT is like a rocket ship
It can take us to new heights and help
us achieve things we never thought possible
– Fei-Fei Li

Hey freelancers, entrepreneurs, and business owners! Imagine yourself several months in the future. You're on a roll and the cash is pouring in. So, what do you do with all that extra dough? It's time to get smart with that loot and start investing in yourself.

Investing in your own skills and knowledge is essential to maintaining your competitive edge. You don't want to be left behind like those sad '90s boy bands, do you? So, allocate some of that extra cheddar towards continuing education, attending conferences, and finding yourself a kickass mentor. Keep up with the trends, and stay fresh like a brand-new pair of Jordans.

But that's not all. You've got to expand your business and start crushing it like a Marvel superhero. Hire some more employees or outsource tasks to help you scale up and take on more massive projects. With more greenbacks, you can launch your business into the stratosphere and build your brand into an empire.

And don't forget about the future. Saving some of that hard-earned cabbage is a must. Set some aside in a savings account or investment portfolio to ensure you're financially secure for whatever life throws your way. Think of it as insurance, in case Thanos snaps his fingers again.

GIVING BACK

But wait, there's more! Giving back is also key to success. Don't be a Scrooge McDuck hoarding all that moola in your vault. Share the love and donate to charity. You'll feel good about doing good, and your community will thank you for it.

There are numerous ways you can pay it forward in addition to charitable donations. Consider volunteering, investing in education, mentoring someone in your industry, or performing random acts of kindness. Paying it forward benefits others but can also bring you personal fulfillment and satisfaction. For more suggestions about paying it forward, enter this prompt…

> *List 15 ways I can pay it forward*

Now, let's explore the ways you can harness the power of ChatGPT to transform your business and earn that money!

BRAINSTORMING

We scratched the surface of brainstorming in Chapter 3. Now, let's take a deeper dive into some amazing ways to use ChatGPT to up your brainstorming game.

OPEN-ENDED QUESTIONS

The easiest way to brainstorm is to ask open-ended questions. This gives ChatGPT room to expand on the question and gets you thinking outside the box. Chances are high that you'll stumble upon a brilliant idea you never would have thought of on your own. Here are some open-ended prompts to get you started…

What should I charge my clients as a freelancer?
What are cost-effective ways to expand my business?
How can I differentiate my startup from my competitors?
How can I improve my business model to increase revenue?
What are some effective marketing strategies for my business?
What are some strategies to promote my services as a freelancer?

AUTO-COMPLETION

Another technique is auto-completion. This is where you start a sentence and let ChatGPT fill in the rest. For example, you could start with "I want to create a product that..." and let ChatGPT work its magic. Check out these auto-completion prompts…

As a freelancer, I want to find new clients by
As a business owner, I want to increase my sales in
As an entrepreneur, I want to create a product that will
As a freelancer, I want to expand my services by offering
As a business owner, I want to reduce my operating costs by
As an entrepreneur, help me develop a new business model that will

GET SILLY

Don't be afraid to get silly with ChatGPT. Sometimes great ideas come from unexpected places. You could ask ChatGPT to generate a list of wacky product names or ask it to come up with a slogan that's completely ridiculous. You might uncover a gem that makes you laugh and inspires you at the same time. Try out these unique prompts…

Suggest interesting ways to find a mentor
List wacky ways I could thank my employees
Brainstorm crazy things I can upsell as a freelancer
What's the craziest thing I can do to market my services?
What are wild ways I can collaborate as an entrepreneur?
What's the most insane customer experience I could provide?

Brainstorming with ChatGPT can be a wild and wacky adventure, but it's also a powerful tool for unlocking your creativity and generating new ideas.

IDEA GENERATION

ChatGPT is invaluable for idea generation. Provide a concise description of your project or the problem you're trying to solve and ChatGPT will produce a diverse array of ideas. Here are some idea-generation prompts…

Propose partnership ideas to help expand my local coffee shop
Generate 10 unique marketing strategies for my online clothing store
Give me some creative suggestions for blog topics related to sustainable living

The use of ChatGPT for idea generation helps foster a fresh perspective and enhances brainstorming, saving you time while expanding your creative horizons.

SCAMPER METHOD

ChatGPT can help implement the SCAMPER method, a proven technique for creative thinking and problem-solving. Enter a description of your product, service, or process, and ask ChatGPT to provide suggestions based on the SCAMPER Method (**S**ubstitute, **C**ombine, **A**dapt, **M**odify, **P**ut to another use, **E**liminate, or **R**everse elements). Type [*Use the SCAMPER method*] before each of the following prompts…

> *To expand opportunities for my web design business*
> *To increase customer acquisition for my marketing agency*
> *To make my eco-friendly product packaging more cost-effective*

You can also specify the aspect of SCAMPER you want to focus on (**S**ubstitute, **C**ombine, **A**dapt, **M**odify, **P**ut to another use, **E**liminate, or **R**everse elements) and provide context about your business or project to get more targeted suggestions.

Using ChatGPT with the SCAMPER method can invigorate your brainstorming sessions, helping you discover unique solutions and enhance your products in ways you haven't considered.

SIX THINKING HATS

Leveraging ChatGPT in conjunction with the Six Thinking Hats method can be a dynamic approach to brainstorming. This method encourages looking at a problem from multiple perspectives represented by different *hats*. ChatGPT is great at simulating the Six Thinking Hats method.

Start by posing questions or scenarios and ask for responses in the guise of each hat - facts (white hat), feelings (red hat), critical judgment (black hat), positive viewpoints (yellow hat), creative ideas (green hat), and process control (blue hat). Type [*Use 6 thinking hats to explore*] before each of the following prompts…

> *Overhauling my company's branding*
> *The possible benefits of a remote work policy*
> *The response of my customers to a price increase*

You can also specify which *hat* you want ChatGPT to *wear*. It will generate responses that align with the particular mode of thinking each hat represents.

By doing so, you'll engage ChatGPT's capacity for diverse thought patterns, enabling a comprehensive analysis of your situation. Using ChatGPT with the Six Thinking Hats can enhance your decision-making process, stimulate creativity, and foster balanced thinking.

SWOT ANALYSIS

Utilizing ChatGPT for conducting a SWOT (**S**trengths, **W**eaknesses, **O**pportunities, **T**hreats) analysis can be a strategic move for businesses and entrepreneurs.

By entering details about your business or project, you can request ChatGPT to analyze and generate insights about potential strengths, weaknesses, opportunities, and threats. This might involve assessing internal factors like operational efficiency, or external factors like market trends. Type [*Generate a SWOT analysis*] before each of the following prompts...

> *Outlining strengths of my mobile app development business*
> *Identifying potential weaknesses in my online bakery's operations*
> *Suggesting opportunities my digital marketing agency could leverage*

Even though ChatGPT is crunching patterns and doesn't exactly have a real-world consciousness, it can still toss out some pretty cool perspectives and insights that you might have missed. Think of ChatGPT as a powerhouse buddy for your SWOT analysis – it's there to lend a hand with your strategic planning and to assist you in navigating the terrain of your professional arena.

TEXT-BASED MIND MAPS

Having ChatGPT create a text-based mind map can be an incredible way to organize thoughts and explore ideas. By initiating a topic or central concept, you can ask ChatGPT to produce related ideas or subtopics. This allows you to expand on the main idea and delve deeper into each subtopic.

Type [*Create a text-based mind map on*] before each of the following prompts...

> *Possible revenue streams for my fitness blog*
> *Different marketing strategies for my new e-book*
> *Potential services I could offer as a freelance web developer*

Even though ChatGPT can't create visual mind maps, it has a knack for generating interconnected ideas that mimic the structure of a mind map in text.

Even without fancy graphics, ChatGPT can help you explore new connections and take your text-based mind mapping to the next level. It'll help expand the depth and richness of your ideas. You can also go the extra mile by asking ChatGPT to dive deeper into specific branches or ideas to expand your text-based mind map further.

INNOVATIVE OFFERINGS

Whether you're a freelancer, entrepreneur, or business owner, staying competitive with the latest products and/or services is key. As a variation on the brainstorming theme, let's explore using ChatGPT to develop innovative offerings, unique products, or services that stand out from the competition and provide value to your customers in a different way.

The first step in developing innovative offerings is to identify the audience you're trying to reach with your product or service? Once you've nailed that down, ask ChatGPT to generate a list of related searches and topics that might appeal to your target audience. With all of ChatGPT's ideas, you'll be grinning like a kid in a candy store. Get your creative juices flowing with these prompts...

> *What's a unique approach I can use as a freelancer?*
> *Can you suggest ways to make my business more innovative?*
> *How can I set myself up to stand out from fellow entrepreneurs?*

Another way to develop innovative offerings is to allow ChatGPT to expand on your existing good ideas. Let's say you've come up with a basic idea for a product but you're not quite sure how to take it to the next level. Ask ChatGPT to help you expand on that idea and give you some new angles to explore.

ChatGPT is also excellent at identifying industry trends. Ask ChatGPT to analyze your industry and identify gaps or opportunities you might take advantage of. Maybe ChatGPT will suggest a new market segment or point out a trend that's ripe for disruption. Now you have a virtual crystal ball that can help you see into the future.

VALIDATING AND REFINING IDEAS

Once you've come up with some innovative offerings, it's time to validate and refine those ideas with market research. Ask ChatGPT to generate a list of related searches and topics that are relevant to your idea and use that information to see if there's a market for your new product. You'll be amazed. ChatGPT is a wiz at identifying trends and patterns in data. Use these prompts to validate and refine your ideas…

> *How can I validate and refine ideas as a freelancer?*
> *What's the best way to refine my entrepreneurial approach?*
> *Suggest ways we can validate and refine our small business model*

For existing products, ChatGPT can serve as your digital Sherlock Holmes, diving deep into the sea of customer feedback to identify those all-important clues - key trends, common hiccups, and emotional undercurrents. ChatGPT sifts through reviews, social media banter, and survey answers, sussing out recurring themes that may give your business a boost or a headache.

For instance, ChatGPT might shine a spotlight on that one feature of your product that's getting more applause than a rockstar at a sold-out concert, or it could flag those grumbles and groans that suggest you need a re-design. ChatGPT can gauge the overall vibe of your customer base, painting a picture of their satisfaction level and emotional state in technicolor. Use these prompts to help analyze customer feedback…

Identify improvements from this webinar feedback
Analyze product return reasons for my e-commerce store
Find themes in social media comments about my vegan pastries

This priceless intel can guide you like GPS through the labyrinth of decisions, helping you make those critical calls on everything from product development to customer service.

In your quest for refinement and validation, consider prompting outside of the box. Sometimes, great ideas come from unexpected places. Ask ChatGPT to generate a list of crazy product ideas or ask it to pitch slogans that are completely off the wall. ChatGPT might deliver a zinger that makes you laugh and inspires you at the same time.

By refining and validating your ideas, you will create products and services that meet your customers needs, resulting in higher customer satisfaction and, you guessed it, increased revenue.

ANALYZING COMPETITORS

What's one of the main obstacles to your success as a freelancer, entrepreneur, or business owner? Competition. ChatGPT can help you analyze your competitors and come up with strategies to beat them in the market. In the previous section, you used ChatGPT to help you analyze from the inside out. Now you're going to switch it up and think from the outside in, starting with your competitors.

Before you start analyzing your competitors, you need to know who they are. Who's offering similar products or services in your market? Ask ChatGPT to generate a list of related businesses or services similar to yours. Once you've figured out who your competitors are, use ChatGPT to analyze their strengths and weaknesses. Let these prompts spark your imagination…

How can I analyze competitors as a freelancer?
List ways I can analyze my entrepreneur competitors
As a small business owner, how can I analyze my competitors?

As you compare yourself to similar businesses, prompt ChatGPT to suggest new features or benefits that no one else is offering. You can also ask ChatGPT to identify a target audience that your competitors might be neglecting.

Once you've identified a weakness in your competitor's product or service, quiz ChatGPT about how to take advantage of it. Ask ChatGPT to expand on that idea and give you some new angles to explore. Use these prompts as a springboard…

> *Modify my product to exploit my competitor's weaknesses*
> *Highlight my competitor's weakness in my marketing campaign*
> *What opportunities arise from this competitor's product weakness?*

Maybe you'll discover a new marketing strategy that targets the weakness, or ChatGPT might help you identify a new feature that fills a gap in the market.

CONTENT CREATION

In the digital age, content is king! For freelancers, entrepreneurs, and business owners, it's the royal road to boosting income. ChatGPT can help you create compelling content that attracts a wider audience and opens up new monetization opportunities.

Take content creation to the next level by deeply understanding your target audience. Use data analytics, feedback, and market research to comprehend their interests, pain points, and desires.

Next, focus on quality over quantity. It's better to produce one piece of stellar content that resonates with your audience and aligns with their needs than ten that fall flat. Content that educates, entertains, or inspires is more likely to be shared, expanding your reach organically. These prompts can get you started…

> *Outline a podcast episode about sustainable living*
> *Generate a list of engaging blog topics for a fitness website*
> *Create a script for a short explainer video about my new mobile app*

Diversify your content forms. Don't just write blog posts. Use ChatGPT to help create videos, podcasts, infographics, webinars, or even e-books. Audiences prefer different types of content and diversity helps you reach a broader base.

Finally, consider monetizing your content directly. If you provide high-value content, you can create premium articles, courses, or digital products for sale. You might also consider affiliate marketing, sponsored content, or advertising revenue. Superior and diverse content that truly serves your audience can open up multiple income streams and elevate your success!

CONCLUSION

In a world where business moves at warp speed and every minute counts, ChatGPT swoops in like a caped crusader to save the day for freelancers, entrepreneurs, and business owners alike. With ChatGPT by your side, you'll be faster than Quicksilver on caffeine, generating ideas and suggestions that are tailor-made for your target audience.

Imagine having a brainstorming session with the Avengers, where Iron Man shares his genius insights, Black Widow offers her strategic prowess, and Thor brings the thunder of creative ideas. That's the power of ChatGPT's machine-learning algorithms.

ChatGPT's ability to process vast amounts of information in record time allows it to unleash a torrent of brilliant ideas. It's like having a super-powered thinking machine on your side, ready to provide you with lightning-fast insights and unleash a storm of creativity. With ChatGPT, you'll never be short on innovative ideas to save the day in your brainstorming sessions.

Seize this opportunity to harness the extraordinary abilities of ChatGPT. With its customized ideation and integration capabilities, you'll soar higher than you ever thought possible. Watch your productivity skyrocket, your workflows become as smooth as butter, and your earnings reach new heights!

KEY TAKEAWAYS FROM CHAPTER 6

- ChatGPT is an amazing brainstorming tool
- Use with SCAMPER, 6 Thinking Hats, and Mind Maps
- ChatGPT helps develop unique products or services
- ChatGPT assists in validating and refining ideas
- ChatGPT helps analyze competitors
- ChatGPT enhances content creation

Get ready for some fun with ChatGPT…

SEVEN
VIRTUAL THEME PARK
FUN WITH CHATGPT

ChatGPT is like a theme park for the mind
A place where you can explore, experiment
and unlock new worlds of wonder and possibility
— Stuart Russell

As a reward for all the effort you've put in and the success you've achieved with ChatGPT, it's time to let loose and have some fun! Welcome to the ChatGPT Theme Park, where the possibilities are as endless as a Marvel movie marathon.

First stop, the **Conversation Carousel**. With ChatGPT as your discussion partner, enjoy endless entertainment and mental stimulation. Engage in imaginative scenarios, create captivating stories, simulate conversations with historical figures, discuss your gaming passions, and delve into deep philosophical debates. The Carousel offers a diverse range of topics to keep your mind buzzing!

Next, take a thrilling ride on the **Roller Coaster to Anywhere**. Get ready for a whirlwind of inspiration as ChatGPT helps you plan your next adventure. Discover new cities, unwind on beaches, or conquer mountains. ChatGPT helps brainstorm ideas and offers budget-friendly destinations. It serves as your virtual tour guide, uncovering local secrets and famous landmarks. Learn about history and culture, get restaurant recommendations, and find unique activities. Let ChatGPT plan your trip and make some unforgettable memories.

Do you love games? Step into the **Game Galaxy** for an immersive gaming experience. Enjoy word games, guessing games, and customized trivia quizzes. Play alone or with friends, tailoring games to your interests. Engage in social deduction games like Werewolf, create role-playing adventures, and challenge your knowledge with personalized trivia. Let ChatGPT be your guide to endless fun and excitement!

If you're up for a mental challenge, enter the **Puzzle Pavilion** for an exhilarating mental journey with ChatGPT. Solve brain teasers, riddles, anagrams, and cryptograms. ChatGPT can even create custom treasure hunts, leading you to hidden treasures and secret locations. Test your mental prowess with intriguing brain teasers and explore word puzzles like word ladders and homophones. Embark on riddle quests filled with humor and clever wordplay. Join the Puzzle Pavilion and unlock your puzzle-solving potential!

Last, but not least... The **Funhouse of Randomness**, where you'll engage in whimsical adventures and explore rooms like the Witty Banter Zone, Chaos Corner, and the Pop Culture Palace. Ask ChatGPT anything, from silly questions to scientific queries, and be entertained by its vast knowledge and sense of humor. Engage in debates, share jokes, and discuss random topics like the best Star Wars movie. Think outside the box and embrace the randomness!

Embrace the fun side of ChatGPT and let your imagination run wild in this virtual theme park. ChatGPT will help you enjoy some well-deserved leisure time. As the great Ferris Bueller once said, "Life moves pretty fast. If you don't stop and look around once in a while, you could miss it." At the ChatGPT Theme Park, you won't miss a thing.

CONVERSATION CAROUSEL

Welcome to the Conversation Carousel, where you can engage in all sorts of discussions with ChatGPT! Whether you're looking for hilarious jokes, magical stories, or conversations with historical figures, ChatGPT is ready to provide endless entertainment and stimulation for your mind.

JOKE GENERATOR

ChatGPT generates jokes, puns, and witty one-liners that will have you laughing out loud. You might even develop your own comedic style after chatting with ChatGPT. Stop kidding around and try these prompts…

How about some puns?
Know any knock-knock jokes?
Tell me some jokes about penguins

HYPOTHETICAL SCENARIOS

If hypothetical scenarios are more your speed, ChatGPT can help you explore different possibilities and outcomes. What if you won the lottery? What if you had superpowers? Let your imagination run wild as you converse with ChatGPT and see where the discussion takes you. Try these prompts…

What if we could swap bodies with animals for a day?
What if dogs could talk, but they only spoke in Pig Latin?
What if everyone had the ability to fly, but only a minute a day?

STORYTIME

Telling stories is another fun way to pass the time on the Conversation Carousel. ChatGPT can help you brainstorm ideas, develop characters, and even generate plot twists that will keep you on the edge of your seat. You might be inspired to write your own novel or screenplay after a few conversations with ChatGPT. Here are some prompts…

Tell me a story about getting lost in a shopping mall
What kind of stories do aliens tell each other about humans?
Come up with a tale about a talking dog who becomes a superhero

PONDERING PHILOSOPHY

If you want a deeper level of conversation, ChatGPT will engage in philosophical discussions about the meaning of life, morality, and other big questions. Contemplate the nature of existence or ponder the role of technology in society. Philosophize with these prompts…

Let's discuss the meaning of life
Let's debate about fate or free will
What's your philosophy on happiness?

STEP BACK IN TIME

Step into a time machine with ChatGPT and have a blast exploring history and popular culture! ChatGPT has an incredible ability to simulate conversations with famous personalities, giving you a chance to chat with legends like Abraham Lincoln, Albert Einstein, Cleopatra, Marilyn Monroe, or Martin Luther King Jr.

Imagine a virtual dialogue with these iconic figures! The conversations are based on historical records and public knowledge, so you get a fascinating glimpse into their minds and perspectives. Get ready to dive into captivating conversations and uncover the hidden depths of historical icons!

Speak as though you're [famous musician]
Simulate a conversation with [name of a famous writer]
I'd like to speak with you in the style of [name a historical figure]

GAME GEEKS

Are you eager to share your latest gaming obsession with someone who understands your passion? Hop on the Conversation Carousel and chat with ChatGPT about your favorite games, characters, and strategies. You might even discover new games and genres you never knew existed. Here are some game prompts…

What are the best skills to have in Apex Legends
I love Fortnite! What are some good strategies to get a Victory Royale?
What are some unusual video game recommendations for a fan of Among Us?

The Conversation Carousel is a fun and engaging way to pass the time and stimulate your mind. With ChatGPT as your conversation partner, you can explore a wide range of topics and scenarios, from hypothetical tall tales and jokes to philosophy and fantastical stories. Hop on the Conversation Carousel and see where the discussion takes you.

ROLLER COASTER TO ANYWHERE

The Roller Coaster to Anywhere is not just any ride, it's the journey of a lifetime. As you navigate the twists and turns, ChatGPT acts as your personal travel guide, offering a range of suggestions for your next adventure. Perhaps you want to explore a new city, relax on a beach, or climb a mountain. Whatever your heart desires, ChatGPT can help you plan the perfect itinerary so you can focus on having fun.

FIND A DESTINATION

Don't know where you want to go? ChatGPT can help you brainstorm possibilities. Are you interested in the world's best culinary destinations, outdoor adventures, cities steeped in history, or just want to take a road trip across the country with friends? ChatGPT can suggest destinations that will blow you away without blowing your budget. Use these prompts for inspiration…

Travel suggestions off the beaten path
I'm in the mood for an adventure! Where should I go?
I want to go somewhere that will make my Instagram followers jealous

DIGITAL TOUR GUIDE

Need a tour guide? ChatGPT is the ultimate host for exploring neighborhoods and cities. It's like having a virtual Rick Steves and Lonely Planet rolled into one. Imagine you're visiting a new city and want to explore some hidden gems that only locals know about, or you want to see the famous landmarks and tourist hotspots. ChatGPT can help you find those magical spots with prompts like these…

Find the weirdest tourist attraction in the area
I heard there's a local market that sells exotic foods
Are there any street festivals going on in the neighborhood?

HISTORY AND CULTURE

ChatGPT can also be a great way to learn about the history of the places you're visiting. Use ChatGPT's vast knowledge to tell you about the origins of a famous landmark or the backstory of a local neighborhood. With ChatGPT as your guide, you'll come away with a greater appreciation for the places you visit. Try these prompts for unique suggestions…

List the most interesting historical sites I should visit
I'm curious about events that shaped this city's history
Can you recommend any good books or documentaries?

VIRTUAL CONCIERGE

ChatGPT is a virtual concierge that can help you find the best restaurants, bars, and cafes. Try local specialties and really get to know the area. With ChatGPT's help, you're sure to find great places to eat and drink. Explore these prompts…

I want to try some authentic local cuisine
Recommend local restaurants or cafes in the area
Suggest a restaurant with an interesting theme or atmosphere

ONLINE ACTIVITY DIRECTOR

Looking for entertainment? ChatGPT will help you find fun and unique activities. Take a bike ride or a walking tour of a historic district. Or visit a local art museum.

ChatGPT can personalize your trip by finding activities tailored to your group's interests. Create a unique experience based on your group's personalities and quirks. ChatGPT will help you maximize your time with activities that are fun and memorable. These prompts are perfect…

Help me find off-the-beaten-path activities
I want to experience the weirdest things in [city name]
Suggest activities that will make me feel like an adventurer

Whether you prefer a relaxed itinerary or an action-packed adventure, ChatGPT will help you plan an amazing trip to make the most of your time. From finding hidden gems to local hotspots, ChatGPT is your ultimate virtual travel companion. Sit back, relax, and let ChatGPT handle the planning while you enjoy your journey.

GAME GALAXY

Welcome to the Game Galaxy, where imagination knows no bounds! ChatGPT is ready to generate word games, guessing games, and personalized trivia quizzes that will keep you entertained for a lifetime. Play against ChatGPT or with friends. Customize games to your skill level and interests. Test out these prompts…

Suggest a game to play with my grandma
I need a fun game to play while waiting for my pizza
I'm feeling a bit wordy today. Can you suggest a game?

GUESSING GAMES GALORE

Looking for a fun game to play with friends or family? ChatGPT will generate guessing games like *20 Questions, 2 Truths & a Lie, Never Have I Ever*, and *Would You Rather*. If you're hosting a game night for friends and family, ChatGPT's guessing games will provide endless entertainment. Try these prompts…

> *Wanna play a game of 20 Questions?*
> *I need some would-you-rather questions*
> *What are some guessing games we can play?*

CUSTOM TRIVIA QUIZZES

Do you love trivia? Look no further than ChatGPT! With its vast knowledge base and customization capabilities, ChatGPT can generate trivia games on any topic, from pop culture to history.

You can even personalize the questions to make it more challenging and engaging. Playing with a group? ChatGPT will generate rules for multiplayer games. Get ready to put your knowledge to the test with ChatGPT trivia! Test your knowledge with these prompts…

> *Create a trivia game about '90s boy bands*
> *Create a trivia about the history of inventions*
> *Create a trivia game about my favorite TV shows*

SOCIAL DEDUCTION GAMES

ChatGPT can take your social deduction experience to the next level with games like *Werewolf* or *Mafia*. Use ChatGPT to generate different scenarios and roles. You can also use ChatGPT to help you strategize and outwit your opponents.

Whether you're playing with family or friends, ChatGPT will provide insights and suggestions to make your game more thrilling and unpredictable. Get ready to sharpen your deduction skills with the help of ChatGPT. Take a shot with these prompts…

What other social deduction games are there?
Let's put our skills to the test with a game of Werewolf
Can you help us keep track of who's who in a game of Mafia?

ROLE PLAYING

Feeling adventurous? Try some role-playing. ChatGPT can help you create characters and scenarios for your very own *Dungeons and Dragons*-style game. ChatGPT can act as a Dungeon Master, setting up scenarios, responding to player actions, and advancing the story in creative and unexpected ways. You'll find yourself battling manticores, exploring mysterious ancient tombs, or embarking on an epic quest. Try these adventurous prompts…

Suggest some fantasy worlds we can create
Let's take on a new persona and role-play a fun scenario
What roles could our role-playing party assume in our campaign?

What are you waiting for? Enter the Game Galaxy and let ChatGPT help you take your gaming to the next level. With customized word games, trivia quizzes, and D&D-style multiplayer experiences, you're sure to have a blast. Just be sure to take breaks for snacks and hydration - I wouldn't want you to get lost in the fun!

PUZZLE PAVILION

If you're up for a mental challenge, the Puzzle Pavilion is the place to be! With ChatGPT at the helm, you'll never run out of brain teasers, riddles, anagrams, and cryptograms. You can even use ChatGPT to create customized treasure hunts, where you solve puzzles and clues to uncover hidden treasure. With ChatGPT's ability to customize and generate unique content, the possibilities for fun and challenging puzzles are incredible!

BRAIN TEASERS

Looking for a good brain workout? ChatGPT has you covered with a variety of mind-bending brain teasers to challenge even the most seasoned puzzler. From complex logic puzzles to tricky lateral puzzles, ChatGPT can generate a wide range of text-based puzzles. So put on your thinking cap and get those neurons firing! Check out these prompts…

I'm in the mood for a fun brain teaser
Help me come up with a brain teaser about dogs
I need a brain teaser to stump my know-it-all friend

WORD PUZZLES

Looking for a captivating mental workout that will twist your words and challenge your linguistic prowess? Let ChatGPT unravel the wonderful world of word puzzles! Explore the fascinating realm of Word Ladders, dive into the arena of Anagrams, crack open a cornucopia of Cryptograms, and tune your ears to the harmonies of Homophones.

ChatGPT will ignite your love for wordplay and take you on an entertaining voyage into the captivating world of word puzzles. Prepare to sharpen your vocabulary, unravel linguistic enigmas, and embark on a thrilling mental adventure like no other! These prompts are your ticket…

Find a palindrome that is a three-letter word
Provide me with an anagram for the word cinema
Construct a word ladder connecting cat to dog in four steps
Create a homophone puzzle using the words night and knight

RIDDLES

Looking for an adventure that will challenge your wit and curiosity? Let ChatGPT be your guide on an exhilarating riddle quest! Embark on a journey of intellectual exploration as you decipher cunning riddles, sprinkled with a dash of humor and some clever dad jokes to keep the excitement alive! Feeling stumped? Fear not! ChatGPT is always ready to help ignite your riddle-solving genius and propel you forward on this thrilling expedition. Riddle me these prompts…

Write a riddle about a haunted house
Do you know a riddle about an old man?
Create a riddle about an animal with spots

CUSTOM TREASURE HUNTS

Looking for a fun way to explore your city or neighborhood? Let ChatGPT help you create a thrilling treasure hunt! Follow the clues, solve the riddles, and uncover hidden treasure in your community. Be prepared for unexpected surprises and laughs along the way - who knows, maybe ChatGPT will throw in a few jokes to keep things interesting! Feeling adventurous? Try these prompts…

Create a treasure hunt for my kids
Plan a treasure hunt in my own backyard
Create a neighborhood treasure hunt with my friends

Come on down to the Puzzle Pavilion and see if you have what it takes to conquer ChatGPT's mind-bending brain teasers, riddles, and treasure hunts. You might even discover a new passion for puzzle-solving!

FUNHOUSE OF RANDOMNESS

The Funhouse of Randomness is the perfect destination for those seeking a lighthearted and unpredictable experience. Leave ordinary at the door as you step into an exhilarating realm where the only constant is change. In this unpredictable playground, around every corner and inside every door, there's a brand new surprise.

With ChatGPT as your guide, you'll navigate a kaleidoscope of unusual and exciting possibilities. In the Funhouse of Randomness, hilarity and spontaneity are the order of the day, making each visit an entirely unique adventure. So let loose, embrace the unexpected, and dive headfirst into the delicious chaos that is the Funhouse of Randomness. Your journey into the beautifully unpredictable awaits.

RANDOM ROOMS

I entered the following prompt…

> *List rooms in the Funhouse of Randomness*

Here are some rooms ChatGPT suggested…

>Pop Culture Palace
>Time Warp Tunnel
>Witty Banter Zone
>Mystery Mansion
>Alien Encounter
>Giggle Gallery
>Chaos Corner
>Babble Booth
>Fantasy Forest
>Mindfulness Maze
>Probability Tunnel
>Hypnotic Chamber
>Quantum Playground
>Whimsical Obstacle Course

To be honest, I have no idea what some of these rooms are, but I'm intrigued, aren't you? I mean, who wouldn't want to check out Chaos Corner, the Probability Tunnel, or the Whimsical Obstacle Course? What are those rooms and what happens inside them? That's the magic of ChatGPT, it generates concepts and ideas that are completely outside the box!

AN INTERESTING OBSERVATION

I asked ChatGPT to brainstorm rides for the ChatGPT Theme Park. It suggested a number of possibilities, including Conversation Carousel, Game Galaxy, Puzzle Pavilion, and the Funhouse of Randomness.

As I was writing the section about the Funhouse of Randomness, I prompted ChatGPT for possible rooms inside the Funhouse. It generated the list I just shared. As I reviewed the list, I noticed the names included words and phrases from previous entries in the chat thread I created to brainstorm this chapter.

This is a real-world example of…

DEEP LEARNING

It's mind-blowing to see evidence of ChatGPT actively learning from my prompts and the responses I select. It's like watching a student gradually become more proficient, improving their ability to produce ideas, suggestions, and content based on the prompts I've been sending their way.

This remarkable feat is due to deep learning, the cutting-edge AI technology that powers ChatGPT. Every single interaction is an experience from which ChatGPT learns and sharpens its skills, continually evolving with each prompt. Speaking of prompts, I cooked up a few that are perfect for the Funhouse of Randomness…

> *What's the most random fact you know?*
> *What's the most random thing you ever heard?*
> *If you could have a random animal as a pet, what would it be?*

You can see from this exercise in randomness that ChatGPT really can help you think outside the box. Way outside the box! This will help you see different perspectives and come up with unique ideas for solving problems and challenges. So, next time you're stuck on something, remember the Funhouse of Randomness at the ChatGPT Theme Park. It's an excellent place to explore.

CONCLUSION

The ChatGPT Theme Park is like Disneyland of the virtual world! Get ready for endless opportunities to flex your brain muscles, discover new travel destinations, and challenge your friends to trivia quizzes.

With ChatGPT leading the way, you can explore virtual versions of theme park worlds like the **Conversation Carousel**, **Roller Coaster to Anywhere**, **Game Galaxy**, **Puzzle Pavilion**, and my favorite, the **Funhouse of Randomness**. It's like having a personalized tour guide take you through the most exciting theme park ever!

The ChatGPT Theme Park isn't just about having fun - it's also a place to expand your horizons and connect with others. ChatGPT creates a personalized and engaging experience that encourages learning and fosters a sense of community. It's like the ultimate combination of entertainment and education - who knew learning could be this fun?

And once your devices are connected through an integration platform, you'll be able to engage with like-minded virtual theme park visitors from around the world, fostering a sense of community and belonging. ChatGPT, where fun and learning collide! You might even discover a new favorite ride!

KEY TAKEAWAYS FROM CHAPTER 7

- ChatGPT engages in amazing conversations
- ChatGPT suggests travel destinations
- ChatGPT generates custom word games and trivia quizzes
- ChatGPT generates a variety of text-based puzzles
- ChatGPT can help you get random and think outside the box!

Let's examine the ethical implications of ChatGPT…

EIGHT
THE MORAL MAZE
ETHICS AND A.I.

ChatGPT is a tool
The choice about how it gets deployed is ours
– Oren Etzioni

Throughout history, technological innovations that were originally developed for good have been hijacked for evil purposes. From the printing press to Artificial Intelligence, each technological advancement has brought about new opportunities and challenges, kind of like when you start playing Fortnite and get addicted to it, and then realize that it's taking over your life.

The printing press, invented in the 15th century, was basically the original meme-making machine. It revolutionized the way information was distributed, enabling publishers to produce books on a massive scale. However, this newfound power also had its downside. Books and pamphlets were soon published as propaganda for political and religious agendas.

The steam engine, invented in the late 18th century, was the OG Tesla - it transformed transportation and manufacturing but also paved the way for factories that exploited workers and spewed pollution into the air, kind of like how Tesla's autopilot feature sometimes crashes into things.

Atomic energy, harnessed through nuclear fission in the 1940s, was like a superhero power - it could be used for good but also had the potential to destroy the world. Kind of like how the Infinity Stones in *The Avengers* could either save the universe or wipe it out.

Genetic engineering, originally developed in the 1970s, has the potential to make us all X-Men with superpowers. But it also raises concerns about the ethics of playing God and the potential for unintended consequences, like in every *Jurassic Park* movie where they create a bunch of dinosaurs and everything goes horribly wrong.

21ST CENTURY INVENTIONS

Social media, a 21st-century phenomenon, brought us unprecedented connectivity and endless cat videos. But it also brought cyberbullying, addiction, fake news, and more targeted ads than we ever thought possible. It's like a high-tech Frankenstein monster, with the power to connect and destroy at the same time.

And now there's AI, the latest technological frontier. It presents amazing opportunities but also has the potential to turn against us, like the movie *Her*, where AI becomes sentient and falls in love with Joaquin Phoenix.

Every technological innovation has its benefits and drawbacks, and it's up to us to ensure that the potential harms are recognized and addressed. By doing so, we can fully harness the benefits of technological innovations while minimizing their negative impacts.

GOVERNMENT REGULATION

The rise of Artificial Intelligence is both exciting and terrifying. It's like watching a movie where you're not quite sure if the robots are the good guys or the bad guys. One thing is for sure: we need government regulation and oversight to protect us from the dangers.

Just like in The Terminator movies, we don't want machines to take over and enslave humanity. We need to ensure that AI is developed and used responsibly, with safety and ethical considerations in mind. We can't rely on tech companies to police themselves, just like we can't rely on a T-800 to make moral decisions.

DANGERS OF AI

The dangers of AI are real. It's like playing with fire - if we're not careful, we'll get burned. From facial recognition technology that can be used for surveillance to autonomous weapons that could cause mass destruction, the potential for harm is enormous. It's like living in a sci-fi dystopia but without the cool gadgets and flying cars.

We need government regulation to ensure that AI is developed in a safe and ethical manner. Just like we have regulations for food safety, environmental protection, and product safety, we need regulations for AI. Otherwise, we're risking a future where we're all at the mercy of Skynet. Let's face it, no one wants to end up like Sarah Connor.

AI'S FULL POTENTIAL

This isn't just about building a fortress against AI's potential pitfalls. It's also about digging into the goldmine of opportunities it offers. Picture this: AI not only helps doctors catch diseases early but also manages traffic better, making your daily commute less of a headache. Imagine AI lending a hand to teachers or helping fight climate change by finding smarter ways to use our resources.

The challenge is striking a balance - enjoying the cool stuff AI can do while making sure AI behaves itself. We need a rulebook to help guide the growth of AI, to make sure we're not unleashing a robot apocalypse on ourselves, and that we're using AI for the greater good.

If the Star Wars gang could save the galaxy time and again, surely we can handle this. So, let's buckle up and may The Force be with us!

CONTACT YOUR CONGRESSPEOPLE

Please contact your congressperson and senators to let them know you want them to support legislation that regulates the development of AI.

Here are websites where you can locate contact information:

> https://www.house.gov/representatives/find-your-representative
> https://www.senate.gov/senators/senators-contact.htm

EMAIL TEMPLATE

Here's a template you can email your congressperson and senators:

Dear [Congressperson's Name]

As a concerned citizen, I am writing to express my support for government regulation and oversight of artificial intelligence (AI). Although AI holds the promise of transforming various facets of our existence, it concurrently presents considerable threats to consumers and the wider society.

Without proper regulation, AI systems could lead to unintended consequences, including job displacement, bias, and privacy violations. We need to ensure that AI is developed and deployed to benefit society as a whole, not just a few corporations or individuals.

I strongly encourage you to back the establishment of legislation that lays down explicit directives for the creation and application of AI, including ethical standards for its design and deployment. Such legislation should provide for oversight and accountability, to ensure AI is used responsibly and transparently.

I appreciate your consideration of this crucial issue. I'm eager to learn about your intended strategies to tackle both the challenges and prospects presented by AI.

Sincerely,

[Your Name]

DATA PRIVACY

Data privacy is a major concern when it comes to AI. Though AI carries the promise to drastically transform various sectors, there are risks and ethical concerns that need to be addressed. One of the main concerns is the protection of personal data. We've all heard of people falling victim to phishing scams and we don't want AI to increase the number of such incidents.

AI-powered tools could also be exploited by malicious individuals or organizations, leading to misuse and potential harm. We need to be cautious with AI, treating it like a babysitter for the Terminator, to prevent any negative consequences.

Surveillance systems powered by AI raise concerns about personal freedoms and privacy rights. Social media platforms, influenced by AI, can amplify divisive content and contribute to societal divisions.

It is crucial for both government and industry to play a vital role in ensuring the safety and security of AI technology. We need to establish safeguards, much like putting up a fence to contain the dinosaurs in Jurassic Park. By working together, we can reap the benefits of AI while mitigating any apocalyptic risks.

USE A SECURE PLATFORM

As you get ready to make your mark in the ChatGPT universe, keep in mind that not everyone is as trustworthy as you are. There are some shady characters out there who use the internet to steal other people's personal information and use it for their own wicked purposes. That's where cybersecurity comes in!

You need to use a secure platform to protect your user data from cyber threats. Trust me, you don't want your personal information to end up in the hands of some villain like Lex Luthor. He'll use it against you like kryptonite!

So, make sure you keep your personal privacy and security in mind when using ChatGPT. Avoid including personal information when creating content with ChatGPT. Stay safe, stay smart, and have fun!

IMPERSONATORS

Can people impersonate others on ChatGPT? You bet they can! It's like a virtual game of *Guess Who?* gone wrong.

With a few cleverly crafted messages, impersonators can channel their inner master of disguise and trick you into thinking they're someone else entirely. It's like the online equivalent of wearing a fake mustache and adopting a fancy accent. But fear not, you have the power of skepticism on your side. Stay sharp and question the suspicious.

There are many ways "AI Impersonators" can show up in your life. Here's how you can spot them…

SUSPICIOUS ENCOUNTERS

One day, you receive a message promising you a lifetime supply of free chocolate if you share your bank details. Hmm, smells fishy, right? That's when your inner Sherlock Holmes kicks in.

Scrutinize your communication channels. Unsolicited messages asking for personal information or urgent requests for help should set off alarm bells. Remember, official entities don't slide into your DMs for sensitive info. Stay sharp!

QUESTIONABLE DETAILS

Watch out for those cunning impersonators and their sneaky email tactics. They'll swap out a single letter or add a suspicious extra domain just to trick you.

It's like a game of Scrabble gone awry. Give those email addresses and URLs a good once-over. Misspellings, variations, or domain dodginess are telltale signs of imposters. Don't let them outwit you!

TRUST YOUR GUT

Your gut feeling is a superpower, my friend. If something seems too good to be true, like winning a private concert with Taylor Swift or inheriting a Nigerian fortune, pause and reflect.

Trust your instincts. Those scammers are as obvious as a dancing elephant in a tutu. If it feels off, run away. Don't let their tricks dupe you into their web of deceit.

ACTIVATE RESEARCH MODE

Fire up your trusty search engine and become the Internet's greatest detective. Conduct a search on these suspicious characters. Look for official statements, news articles, or any crumbs of truth that confirm their legitimacy. Remember, real celebrities have fan pages, not just a single follower named "NotARandomImposter2023".

REPORT IMPERSONATORS

If you've unmasked an impersonator or suspect foul play, don't hesitate to report it. Be a superhero and help protect others from falling victim to these scoundrels. Social media platforms and websites have reporting options for a reason.

It's your civic duty to bring these imposters down! Armed with a dash of skepticism, you're equipped to spot sneaky impersonators. Stay vigilant, protect yourself, and keep the internet a safer place.

HATE SPEECH

ChatGPT is designed to follow strict guidelines around hate speech, violent rhetoric, and harmful behavior. It's programmed to not generate, endorse, or promote content that is violent, harmful, or offensive, including hate speech, harassment, or discrimination towards individuals or groups based on attributes such as race, religion, gender, age, nationality, or sexual orientation.

ChatGPT is also not supposed to generate content that encourages or incites violence or any illegal activities. OpenAI's use-case policy explicitly forbids using the AI model in any way that infringes upon the rights of others or that may lead to harm. Misuse can result in restrictions or bans from the service.

However, as an AI model, ChatGPT's understanding is based on patterns in the data it was trained on, and it doesn't comprehend content in the same way humans do. It might inadvertently generate inappropriate responses in certain contexts despite these guidelines. This is called…

BIAS

ChatGPT can sometimes exhibit bias in the responses based on the data it was trained on. That means ChatGPT picked up some bias along the way. These biases might include gender, race, culture, politics, and more.

ChatGPT needs some help correcting its biases. It's important to correct any biases you come across. Think of it like training a puppy not to chew on your favorite shoes - you need to be consistent and patient. Here are some of the most prevalent biases:

- Gender bias: Making assumptions about gender roles
- Racial bias: Using racially derogatory words
- Political bias: Using politically biased language
- Cultural bias: Biases based on references from training data

REPORTING BIASES

If you encounter biases or problematic responses here are some ways to report them:

- OpenAI values user feedback and actively encourages users to report any biases or issues they come across. Reach out

through the OpenAI platform to share your concerns and provide specific examples.
- If you come across biased or inappropriate responses during a conversation, you can flag them within the interface you're using. Most platforms that integrate ChatGPT have mechanisms to report problematic content directly.
- When reporting biases, be specific and provide clear examples of the problematic responses you encountered. Explain why you believe the responses are biased or inappropriate, highlighting any specific concerns you have.

Remember, ChatGPT was trained on a vast amount of text from the internet, and it may inadvertently reflect biases present in that data. OpenAI is actively working on addressing these concerns and improving the system. User feedback plays a crucial role in this ongoing process, so your input is valuable in helping make the model better and more inclusive.

TRANSPARENCY

Are you using ChatGPT to generate amazing content? That's awesome! Are you being transparent about it? Or are you pulling a fast one on your audience?

Unfortunately, some people use ChatGPT to generate content without letting others know that it's not human-generated. That's like trying to pass off a fake Louis Vuitton bag as the real deal!

So, please, be transparent about your use of ChatGPT. Let others know when you're using it to generate content, so they're not left wondering whether they're talking to a person or a machine. It helps build trust with your audience.

Plus, being transparent can actually be a good thing. It shows that you're on the cutting edge of technology, like the Ghostbusters with their proton packs. And who doesn't want to be as cool as the Ghostbusters?

PLAGIARIZATION

It's great to hear that you're using ChatGPT to create awesome content! But keep in mind that some people use the internet to plagiarize, and that's not cool. It's important to respect the intellectual property rights of others.

So, don't use ChatGPT to plagiarize someone else's work. Instead, use it to generate ideas and get inspired to create something that's all you. You can be the Beyoncé of your own universe, creating content that's fresh and original. Put your personal spin on things and make it your own. Who knows? Maybe you'll create the next viral sensation that everyone wants to copy.

CONCLUSION

ChatGPT can be a real game-changer when used properly. To avoid any negative consequences, keep these best practices in mind…

Government plays a critical role in addressing the risks and ethical concerns associated with AI. Regulations are necessary to protect against job displacement, bias, privacy violations, and the potential misuse of AI-powered tools.

Data privacy is another major concern that should be addressed. It's imperative to ensure secure platforms and robust protection against impersonators and scammers. We need to be cautious with AI to prevent any negative consequences.

Combating hate speech and bias in ChatGPT responses is vital for creating an inclusive and respectful environment. By adhering to strict guidelines, we can mitigate the potential harm caused by ChatGPT-generated content.

Transparency about the use of ChatGPT and respecting intellectual property rights are also essential. Openly acknowledging the involvement of ChatGPT in content generation builds trust with the audience, while respecting the creativity and work of others.

By navigating these challenges responsibly and implementing effective regulations, we can use ChatGPT for the fun stuff! ChatGPT can help you create amazing content. It's like having the creativity of Banksy or the humor of Jimmy Fallon at your fingertips. So unleash your imagination and make the most of this incredible technology!

KEY TAKEAWAYS FROM CHAPTER 8

- Government regulation of ChatGPT is necessary
- Use a secure platform to protect your data and privacy
- Impersonating others on ChatGPT is unethical and illegal
- Hate speech and promoting violence are strictly prohibited
- ChatGPT can exhibit biases
- Transparency is key when using ChatGPT to generate content

In the final chapter, we'll explore possibilities for your future…

NINE
THE FUTURE OF POSSIBILITY
CHATGPT AND YOUR FUTURE

The best way to predict the future is to invent it
– Alan Kay

At this point, you must be bubbling with excitement about ChatGPT - the technological revolution that's happening right before your eyes! Imagine being one of the early humans who discovered fire or the Wright brothers when they made their first flight. You're sitting in a front-row seat to the future, where possibilities are as limitless as the galaxies in our universe.

But why wait for the future? With the simple steps in this book, you'll accelerate your journey to ChatGPT mastery faster than the Road Runner on a caffeine high.

Implement the recommendations in this book and you'll know more about ChatGPT than 99% of the rest of the world.

Seize the day and unleash the full potential of ChatGPT! Don't wait for the future to come to you - grab it by the reins and ride it into a new era of innovation. Adventure awaits!

MASTERY

Congratulations! You've achieved a high level of mastery in ChatGPT, having progressed through countless challenges and obstacles. Remember when you first started this journey? The thought of reaching this level seemed like a distant dream. But here you are with a wealth of knowledge and experience at your fingertips.

Let's remember what got you here in the first place - the 5 Easy Steps: **learn**, **apply**, **assess**, **refine**, and **repeat**. These steps have served as your roadmap to success, guiding you through the countless levels and challenges that led you to where you are now.

You might be wondering, "What's next?" The answer is simple: keep going! Just like *Candy Crush*, there's always another level to conquer. And each level brings new experiences, opportunities, and indescribable rewards. Discover new levels of ChatGPT with these prompts…

Instruct me to ask ChatGPT for a structured plan
Explore ChatGPT's capability to create context-specific content
How can I use ChatGPT's ability to construct persuasive arguments

Keep moving forward like Pac-Man, gobbling up new skills and knowledge. Remember the 5 Easy Steps and use them to overcome new challenges that come your way. As you ascend to higher levels, your skills, knowledge, and experience will compound exponentially, opening doors of opportunity you never knew existed.

HONE YOUR PROMPT SKILLS

As you progress on your journey with ChatGPT, you'll come to realize the importance of honing your prompt skills. The more you get to know ChatGPT and what it can do, the better you'll understand how to get the responses you're looking for. You'll try out different ways of structuring your prompts, fine-tune your instructions, and ask questions with precision. As you sharpen your prompt skills, you'll have more meaningful and productive conversations. Dive into these prompts for inspiration…

What's the best way to craft an effective prompt?
Is there a formula for generating output in outline format?
Do you have any advanced tips for crafting more effective prompts?

Effective prompts showcase your creativity. It's like being an artist with a paintbrush, except you're creating a masterpiece with words. You can infuse humor, personality, and even references to your favorite movies or TV shows. Imagine adding Deadpool's wit and charm to the conversation - entertaining, engaging, and unforgettable.

INTEGRATION

As you continue to sharpen your prompt skills, you'll discover the immense potential of integrating ChatGPT seamlessly into your devices and workflow. With each interaction, you'll find new ways to leverage the power of ChatGPT to streamline tasks and enhance productivity. Whether it's automating repetitive processes, generating creative content, or obtaining valuable insights, ChatGPT will become an indispensable tool in your digital arsenal.

Integrating ChatGPT with your apps is like leveling up your character in a role-playing game - you gain new abilities and become a force to be reckoned with. From scheduling appointments to managing tasks, ChatGPT becomes an invaluable sidekick that helps you conquer the digital realm. Unlock ideas with these prompts…

Should I integrate ChatGPT with my devices?
What's an easy way to integrate ChatGPT with my devices?
Is there a more advanced way of integrating ChatGPT into my life?

Integrating ChatGPT with your apps unleashes your creativity. It's like adding a dash of Willy Wonka's magic to your digital experiences - unexpected, delightful, and full of surprises. You can create unique interactions, personalized experiences, and even bring your favorite fictional characters to life through ChatGPT-powered conversations. Refer to Chapter 5 for details about integration services.

COMPLEX TASKS

Everything in the world of ChatGPT is interconnected. It's like a web where each strand is intertwined with the others. As you get better at asking questions, you'll naturally progress to integrating ChatGPT seamlessly into your devices and workflow. And that's where the real magic happens!

Once you've integrated ChatGPT into your life, a whole new world of possibilities opens up. You'll be able to take on more complex tasks. Break free with these prompts…

> *How can I use ChatGPT to attack complex tasks?*
> *Can I use ChatGPT to break complex tasks into smaller bits?*
> *Tell me about a range of complex tasks you've helped people conquer*

Think of the process as a continuous loop. Each step you take builds upon the previous one, leading you closer to unlocking the full potential of ChatGPT. You'll keep discovering new capabilities and exploring the possibilities of what ChatGPT can do. So, embrace the interconnected nature of your journey and let each stage propel you forward. With ChatGPT as your ally, there's no limit to what you can achieve!

COLLABORATE

As you master using ChatGPT for complex tasks, you'll naturally find yourself drawn to collaborating with other ChatGPT enthusiasts. Collaboration is a game-changer!

Imagine your collaboration is a heist from *Ocean's Eleven*. You gather a diverse crew, each with their own expertise, to pull off the impossible. With other ChatGPT enthusiasts by your side, you become Danny

Ocean, orchestrating brilliant conversations and achieving remarkable outcomes. Jumpstart collaboration with these prompts…

What are the benefits of collaborating?
How can I turbocharge my collaboration with others?
What are some strategies for making small groups work together?

Imagine the possibilities when you team up with other ChatGPT enthusiasts. Together, you can push the boundaries of what's possible with ChatGPT and take on even more ambitious projects. It's a chance to contribute to the advancement and exploration of this transformative technology.

So, don't hesitate to embrace the opportunity to collaborate. It's where ChatGPT comes to life. Together, you'll unlock new levels of creativity, expand your horizons, and make a real impact in the world of AI. Get ready to join forces and let the future unfold!

SKILL STACKING

As you delve deeper into the capabilities of ChatGPT, you'll discover the incredible potential of integrating it with your existing knowledge and talents. It's like combining different superpowers to create something truly extraordinary. Take marketing, for example. By combining your expertise with ChatGPT's content creation, you can transform your communication and boost customer engagement.

This powerful combination is called skill stacking, and it's not just for individuals. In a collaborative setting, each team member brings their unique skills to the table, working with ChatGPT to tackle complex projects with greater efficiency and creativity. Get started skill stacking with these prompts…

How can I practice skill stacking?
Tell me about the benefits of skill stacking
Does skill stacking work when I'm collaborating?

Skill stacking allows you to unleash ChatGPT's full potential, empowering yourself or your team to achieve extraordinary results that go beyond what individuals can accomplish alone. So, embrace the power of skill stacking and witness how ChatGPT becomes a catalyst for innovation and success!

CHATBOTS

By now, you've become an expert in harnessing ChatGPT to boost productivity, streamline tedious tasks, craft captivating content, and maximize your bottom line. Now, it's time for you to make the next big leap: chatbots! What the heck is a chatbot?

Chatbots are AI-powered apps that can have virtual conversations with humans. Whether you're chatting on a messaging app, website, or a mobile app, chatbots are used to make communication more efficient and convenient.

Chatbots use LLMs (Large Language Models) to understand what you're saying and respond in a way that feels just like a real person. They automate customer support, give you personalized recommendations, and even make business processes smoother.

These digital wonders are advanced versions of ChatGPT, equipped with extraordinary multitasking skills, 24/7 availability, and the capacity to handle customer interactions with finesse. Let's embark on a journey into the fascinating realm of chatbots—a world where technology and conversation intersect in the most delightful and efficient ways imaginable.

ALWAYS AVAILABLE

Picture a world where customer support never sleeps, where inquiries vanish faster than a magician's rabbit. That's the magic of chatbots! These digital marvels are on-call 24/7, ready to rescue customers from the abyss of unanswered questions. It's like having a customer service superhero that never needs a coffee break.

CUSTOMER SUPPORT

Gone are the days of support teams drowning in an ocean of emails and messages. Say hello to chatbots, the ultimate support superheroes! With lightning-fast responses and an encyclopedic knowledge of FAQs, they swoop in to save the day. It's like having a squad of knowledgeable sidekicks who never miss a beat.

THE POWER OF PERSONALIZATION

One size doesn't fit all—except when it comes to socks. Chatbots understand this too! They collect customer data and preferences, crafting personalized experiences like a digital matchmaker. It's like having a virtual genie who grants wishes for tailored recommendations and custom-tailored responses.

SCALING NEW HEIGHTS

Scaling a business can feel like wrestling a greased pig in a crowded stadium. But fear not, chatbots are here to lend a helping hand! With their multitasking prowess, chatbots handle multiple conversations like a symphony conductor juggling flaming batons. It's like having an army of little helpers that keep your business humming.

STREAMLINING OPERATIONS

Imagine a world where tedious tasks vanish quicker than ice cream on a hot summer day. Enter chatbots, the masters of automation! From scheduling appointments to organizing data, they're like the Swiss Army knives of business operations, freeing you to focus on the tasks that truly light your entrepreneurial fire.

INSIGHT ANALYSIS

Hidden within the chatbot's digital brain lies a treasure trove of insights. It's like a secret underground lair filled with valuable data. By deciphering these chat conversations, you'll unlock the mysteries of customer preferences, their deepest desires, and the occasional love for cat GIFs. It's like being Sherlock Holmes with a knack for understanding customer behavior.

THE HUMAN TOUCH

Chatbots may be superpowered, but they know when to call in the human cavalry. When things get too complex or require a personal touch, they gracefully pass the baton to real-life heroes—your amazing human team. It's like a seamless dance between bots and humans, ensuring a customer experience that's part technology, part humanity, and all-around awesome.

CONCLUSION

Congratulations! You've reached the end of the book. But the journey doesn't stop here. ChatGPT Mastery is an ongoing process. While this book provided you with a solid foundation, there's still much for you to discover.

ChatGPT isn't just a tool or a program; it's a gateway to a new era of creativity, efficiency, and innovation. The 5 Easy Steps - learn, apply, assess, refine, and repeat - helped you overcome challenges and expand your capabilities. Now, armed with that knowledge and experience, you're ready to explore uncharted territories.

But remember, the journey isn't just about reaching the destination; it's about the joy of the journey itself. The joy of discovering new insights, the joy of honing your skills, and the joy of witnessing the transformative power of ChatGPT unfold before your eyes.

As you continue on this journey, you'll unlock even greater potential, create innovative solutions, and make a lasting impact in the world. So, step forward with confidence and a sense of wonder. The future of possibility awaits and ChatGPT is your trusty companion, ready to embark on this extraordinary adventure.

KEY TAKEAWAYS FROM CHAPTER 9

- Continue to hone your prompt skills
- Enhance integration of ChatGPT with your devices and apps
- Explore interconnected capabilities and complex tasks
- Collaborate and skill stack for extraordinary results
- Harness the power of chatbots
- Continue exploring and experimenting

Printed in Great Britain
by Amazon